Her Dating Coach

By Jacob Lucas

ISBN: 978-1-3999-4926-2

Cover design by: Adrianna Kloeckner

Introduction

Welcome to *Her Dating Coach*. I am your Professional Dating Coach, Jacob Lucas. It is my absolute pleasure to meet you.

There may be many different reasons why you chose to read this book... It could be that you are looking for love... Perhaps you are currently in a relationship and want some advice... Maybe you want to know how to flirt with the man that you are going on a date with tomorrow night... Whatever the reason is, I am confident that you will find the guidance that you are looking for in this book.

In this book there will be advice on how to flirt, how to build confidence, what red and green flags to look out for on a date, how to make yourself as attractive as possible, how to maintain a healthy relationship, and so much more!

The guidance in this book uses psychology, social dynamics and knowledge from real life experiences to help you navigate the world of dating and relationships. The advice in this book is worded and structured in a way that's easy to understand and easy to put to practical use in your real-life situations. I want you to imagine it as you are getting advice from your very own personal Dating Coach who has ALL the answers to your questions about your love life.

I am sure that you will love every moment of reading this book. You'll be wondering how you ever lived without it!

To use this book couldn't be any easier. All you need to do is head to the '**CONTENTS**' pages to find the chapter and that you'd like guidance on, and read the knowledge within this book to help you achieve the happiness and success in your love life that you deserve.

Your love story with *Her Dating Coach* to guide you begins now...

Contents

3 Questions to Ask Yourself Before you Start Dating

When dating you always want to give yourself the best possible chance of finding happiness and love. Before you begin your dating journey this is why you need to ask yourself these 3 questions that are in this chapter. Once you know the answers to these questions, you will be laying the correct foundations to finding your forever partner...

Why am I Dating?

The first question that you need to ask yourself when dating is, 'Why am I dating?' This is very important because it sets your whole dating journey's course to move into the direction that you want it too.

Are you looking for a relationship? Do you want to keep things casual? Or are you undecided on why you are dating?

You need to know exactly why you are dating and what you are looking for, because even though the algorithms and psychology of dating remain the same, your perspective of what dating is will vastly differ from someone else who has different dating goals compared to your own.

Let's say you are looking for a relationship; your dating journey is going to vastly differ from someone who wants something casual.

In my opinion, I believe looking for a relationship is far better for you than searching for something casual, and this is why...

If you're having a casual relationship with someone (you meet up here and there, have sex occasionally, and text each other sometimes) and then your perfect man comes into your life who is looking to properly date you... then there's absolutely no way you'd refuse him! You'd jump at the opportunity to be in a relationship with your perfect man instead of something casual with a guy who you don't see a future with.

The reason I am saying this is because if you are tied up in casual relationships, you are spending time with someone you don't see a future with. And whilst you're doing that, you could miss your chance to be with the man of your dreams because you're talking, spending time with, and having sex with someone who you don't really care about. And that's a real shame. But the choice is yours. If you want something casual, just know that you may be missing out on the opportunity to be with a man who is perfect for you.

Now, let's say you are undecided about what you're

looking for... I want you to view dating like this... View dating as a river. One side of the riverbank is 'Looking for a relationship', the other side is 'Looking for something casual'.

If you are firmly on either side of the riverbank, on dry land, then you'll know what you're looking for and will be able to regulate your emotions far better because you know what you are getting into with people, and the rules of your dating life will be clearly defined.

Now, let's say that you're undecided and you're not on either side of the river. There's only one place for you... In the water and you'll end up drowning.

This is because if you kind of want a relationship, then you end up dating someone who wants something casual, then you'll catch feelings for someone who doesn't want to commit to you. Then when they leave you, you'll be questioning your own self-worth and wondering what you did wrong.

If you want to keep things casual but the man you are dating wants a relationship, then he will become needy, and you'll lose attraction for him, and then you'll have to hurt his feelings by rejecting him.

So, you need to pick one side or the other to keep yourself from drowning in that river!

Once you've figured out what you are looking for, you can then move forward with a clearer goal in mind and date like-minded people and save yourself A LOT of time!

What type of man do I

want to be with?

Before you start dating, knowing the type of man that you want to be with is very important. This will save you a lot of time and help you to filter out the guys that you DON'T want to date!

A few examples of the things you need to consider are:

- Age
- Traits that you find physically attractive
- Whether you want someone local or someone who can do long distance
- Yours and their life goals, and dating goals (to see if they align)
- Levels of intelligence
- Lifestyle
- Do they want children or not?

And pretty much anything else that you consider MUST haves when dating someone! The list could be endless. But all that matters is that these people have the desirable traits that you are looking for in a partner.

Once you know exactly what you are looking for, you will then have a clearer vision of the type of person you really should be dating. This way, you won't be wasting time on people who don't align with what you want in a partner. Instead, you'll have a much higher chance of success with someone you are dating who fits the criteria of what you want in a partner because there won't be any fundamentals holding you back. So, I highly suggest that in your mind, or written down, that you have this clear list of criteria and fundamentals that a man must have before you start dating.

I will also say this... You need to be flexible when dating. Someone may have a lot of things you are looking for, BUT not everything.

For example, someone could have 7 out of the 10 things you are looking for, and that's ok to date them if the 3 things that they don't have is something that isn't a dealbreaker for you.

However, someone could have 9 out of 10 things that you want in a partner, BUT if the one thing they don't have is a complete deal breaker for you, then you don't need to be flexible if that trait is a MUST have in a partner; so, you don't need to be open minded about dating them.

Be very clear about what you can and can't live without; and pay close attention to the people you are dating so you don't fail to recognise any of these deal breakers down the line.

One more point I will make about topic is this... Even though you have the criteria of what you need in a partner, when you are out there dating, your type may change a lot! If you meet someone who isn't your usual type, yet you feel drawn towards them, still give that person a chance even if they don't suit the usual type of man that you find attractive. That feeling you have of feeling drawn towards them is something that you shouldn't ignore! Your true type might be someone you never considered before!

Have a clear type of person that you want to date in your mind, but always remember to stay flexible when searching for love...

What are my boundaries?

When dating you MUST be perfectly clear on what your boundaries are. Your boundaries are things that you do and don't find acceptable. And they also protect you! This can range from how someone talks to you, to the way that someone touches you. You set these boundaries not only for someone else to understand, but for yourself to understand!

If you aren't clear on what your boundaries are then you will face a whole world of problems when dating.

- You need to know what your boundaries are that people shouldn't cross even one time.

- Your boundaries where you give someone a warning and see if they back off.

- And your boundaries where you will give someone a couple of chances to correct their behaviour, but no more than that.

Once you have this in your mind, you can then be aware of when you can be dismissive to someone or perhaps give them a second chance.

But do not compromise your boundaries because you are worried if someone likes you or not. These are your boundaries for a reason and don't let anyone manipulate you into letting your guard down and changing your boundaries for their own benefit.

When you first start talking to someone, you don't have to outwardly say to them, 'This is my list of boundaries of what I do and don't accept.' That would come across as very strange. Instead, know what your boundaries are and act accordingly to how the other person behaves towards you.

If they break an unforgivable boundary, don't talk to that person again.

If they break a boundary of yours that can be forgiven because they weren't aware that was a boundary you had, then politely tell them. If they back off, then great. They may simply have been unaware that this behaviour of theirs broke a boundary of yours. And if they apologise and don't repeat it again, then that's ok.

But, if they ignore what you have said about your boundaries and continue their negative behaviours, then pull away from them in every sense of the word.

Once you have a firm understanding of what you do and don't find acceptable, then you are providing yourself with a valuable tool when dating. Not only will it help you find someone who is right for you, but it will give you a power that people can't take away from you.

Where to Meet People

This is one of the biggest questions in Dating! 'Where can I meet new people who are single?!'

There are so many places where you can meet people. The main thing to remember is, 'You can't be found if you can't be seen'. The first thing you need to do is put yourself in positions where people can meet you. If you're expecting the person of your dreams to walk up to your front door, knock on it and expect to fall deeply in love with you, well let's just say, that's never going to happen. You get out what you put into dating. And if you put yourself out there in a position where people can meet you, you are already beating every person out there who isn't even trying.

In this section I'm going to give you a few tips and places which will definitely help you meet new people AND give other people the opportunity to meet you...

Meeting people online

Love it or hate it, online dating is by far one of the easiest ways of meeting single people like yourself. Online dating sometimes has a bad reputation of men just wanting to meet you to have sex with you. And yes, unfortunately you do sometimes come across these types of men. But if you know what to look out for then you can shut down these types of men fast and easily, so you won't be wasting your time even talking to these men.

Dating apps are a fantastic and easy way of meeting single people who are looking to date. Don't be closed off to the idea of joining a dating app because of your friend who said they had a bad experience on it. I know so many people who have met their long-term partners on a dating app. Like I said before, just be careful navigating dating apps and be alert to the types of men who just want sex and will waste your time. Do this correctly and you'll be wondering why you never joined dating apps sooner because there are some great guys on them! Dating apps are fun and exciting if you know what you're looking for.

Also, never underestimate the power that your social media can have when dating. You can meet so many great people on social media. If your social media looks good, people will naturally be attracted to your page and want to talk to you. Just be engaging with other people's pages and you'll be shocked at how amazingly easy it is to connect with potential dates on there.

Think of it like this... You have millions of people at your fingertips. This hasn't been available to us as humankind until recently. Think of it as a good thing!

Embrace your hobbies to meet someone like you

I love this tip. Embrace your hobbies to meet someone like you. What I mean by this is; let's say you are someone who loves the gym... Then go to the gym and start talking to people who also go there! If you like art, start going to art galleries and workshops. If you like cooking, go to cooking classes. All of these are fun things to do, and you will meet like-minded people in an organic way.

I used to run a fitness class when I was younger and the amount of people who met through the fitness class and started dating was a lot more than you might expect. This is because they were in an environment where they were having fun, being social, and with people who had the same interests as themselves. They associated each other with positive emotions because they met doing something they enjoy. They always had something to talk about as well because they were obviously into the same hobbies. Do something you enjoy and meet new people at the same time.

And on a side note... A lot of single people do these sorts of activities and really embrace their hobbies because they have more free time. It's a great way to meet someone amazing who has the same interests as you in an organic way.

We met through a mutual friend

This is a story we have all heard so many couples tell us about when they tell us how they met.

Meeting through a friend can be a fantastic way of meeting new people. Sometimes your friend may be having a party, sometimes they are going out on the town and invite you and some of their other friends along, or sometimes they just have a feeling that you and someone else will hit it off.

Your friends will usually have your best interests at heart, and they will want to match you with someone they think would be a good match for you, and someone who will treat you right. If your friend is very social and someone who always invites you to go out, then do it! You never know who you may meet.

This tip even applies to their social media. You could be tagged in a photo of theirs or leave a comment on one of their posts. Then you never know who is going to see it on your friend's page. They might think you look hot, then drop you a message because they have seen you on your mutual friend's page.

Use your friends as a network to meet new people. When you all start doing this as a friendship group, you can meet some great people that you wouldn't have without the help of your friends.

The key to meeting people organically

Lots of people say meeting people organically can be tough. But if you know what to do it doesn't need to be. I always think of meeting new people organically as a domino effect. Yes, at the start it can be very tough because you don't where to start or how to begin, or you just don't know any new people. And that's ok if this applies to you because many people are in the same situation. But, doing this will definitely help you...

Make yourself as social as possible! Put yourself into lots of different social situations, different activities, or different situations at work. This will give you the opportunity to meet people you wouldn't have normally met. Also, something that is very important to realise is the domino effect that it has. Meeting people who you don't have any attraction to, but you really enjoy their company, could give you the opportunity to meet someone they might know who you do find attractive. Or they may invite you along to something where you meet someone who you end up dating.

Life has a funny way of working out when you open up and say yes to putting yourself out there. And when you meet people organically like this, it usually comes from the most unlikely of places and you'll look back and realise you would have never met them if you didn't say yes to going to a certain place. Being as social possible is key to casting your dating net far and wide!

Dating people from work

Dating people at work can be very tricky. If it goes bad, it can go VERY bad and it's not healthy for your mindset. However, if it goes well, then it can be something very special because you get to see your favourite person every day. BUT there are some rules that you need to follow when dating people in the workplace.

Rule 1

'Get to know that person as a friend before you start dating them.'

Lots of people see someone at work who they find attractive and start dating them and having a sexual relationship with them straight away. Then it ends, and they are left with a lot of hostile feelings towards each other and every day at work becomes a nightmare.

This is because they didn't get to fully know each other and take the time to see if they are compatible on every level. Such as, what they are looking for long term, do their morals align, are there any deal breakers they didn't see at first etc. But if you get to know someone at work fully before you start dating them, and you find out everything aligns, then you can be amazing friends as well as lovers, and that works great!

Rule 2

'Make sure they don't have a history with anyone else in the workplace.'

This can be an absolute disaster if they do for two reasons...

The 1st reason is one of them may still have feelings for the other and before you know it, you'll be stuck in a love triangle at work. That's not a place you want to be.

The 2nd reason is because people tend to repeat patterns they display in their life. If they've done it before, they are likely to do it again. So, let's say a guy has been with someone in the office before you, then he gets with you; if you two end, I almost guarantee he will try to get with another person from the office. Then that opens up a whole other world of problems.

So, make sure he hasn't been with anyone else in the workplace before you.

Rule 3

'Keep your private life private.'

If you're a couple at work, people will always try to poke their nose into your business, and it can cause a lot of friction in the workplace. Remain professional around each other and your work colleges and set very clear boundaries with each other and others around you. Do this and it will help massively. But, if you want to find a secret place at work, away from others, to get intimate together, then do it! That can be very hot and sexy!

Rule 4

'Don't take work home with you.'

Your relationship should be your escape from your professional life. When you get home, try not to talk about work with each other. Unless it's about the time you secretly got intimate with each other in the workplace!

Talk about other things going on in your life. If you always talk about work, it will stress you out and you'll start associating your love life with work, and it will feel like there is no escape from work. Make time to go on dates and do things that couples should be doing that have nothing to do with work!

Do all of these things and a relationship in the workplace

can work very well!

Online Dating

In today's world, online dating is a very important part of dating that you need to know in order to give yourself the best chance of meeting the right person. It can be very tricky to navigate online dating if you don't know what you're doing, but have no fear, I am here to help you with this new modern approach to dating.

Lots of people are closed off to meeting people online and would rather meet people in a more organic setting. I agree meeting people organically can be great, but your life partner is waiting for you out there somewhere, and if you don't put yourself out there on online dating apps or dating websites then you may never meet them! It doesn't matter where you meet 'The One'. The goal is that you meet them, and sometimes this can only be done online. So, I'm going to give you some tips that will give you the best chance of meeting that special someone online...

Dating Apps

Love them or hate them, Dating Apps are a fantastic way of meeting people. Throughout the history of humankind, we've never had such a convenient way of meeting so many people that are single! Yes, you can come across some strange individuals on them, however, don't let the few ruin it for the many. There are many great people on dating apps, and you never know, your future life partner could be one swipe away.

When you go onto a dating app, you need to think about how you can best present yourself in a way that will make people want to talk to you. You can be the funniest, nicest, most interesting person alive, but if you don't make that first impression a good one, then people won't give you the chance to get to know you and find out what a catch you are!

Follow these simple rules and you'll have much more success on Dating Apps...

Your Photos

Your photos will have a big impact on whether you're successful or not on dating apps. You can be the best-looking person alive, but if you're photos aren't looking good, then you're looks won't count for much.

Photos are so important on dating apps because you have around 3 seconds to make an impact on someone. Men are notoriously fast at scrolling through dating apps, and if they don't like your profile photo within the first 3 seconds, they will scroll straight past you. Your profile photo (the first picture on your profile that everyone sees) needs to be the best photo you have of yourself where you look your hottest. Good angles, good lighting and most importantly a BIG smile!

The smile will make you much more approachable to people. If you struggle with what angles to use and how to get good lighting, YouTube, Instagram and TikTok tutorials are amazing for this. But, no matter what, that first photo needs to look good. You don't need to get professional photos. The camera on your phone is all you need.

Profile Photos that you must not use

So, let's get into the types of profile photos that you need to avoid...

The Group Photo

First of all, it's the group photo. I'll be brutally honest, if you put up a group photo, every man assumes you're the person who looks the worst. You may actually be the hottest person in the group photo, however, most men will assume you're the worst and will swipe past you because they think you are using the group photo to hide what you really look like by using the cover of your friends.

Activity Photos

Avoid photos where you're doing an activity (sports etc) unless you look really hot in it. This is because men will look to see if you're hot in those first 3 seconds, and most people doing activities and sports don't look great in photos. You may think it makes you look interesting, and it does, but put those photos more towards the end of your profile because men will go for looks first, then if they get past the first photo and think you look hot, they will want to find out if you're interesting or not.

Other Types of Photos to use in your Dating App Profile

Ok, let's get into what other photos to use in your profile after they've seen the profile photo...

It's good to have a mix of photos and to always give people something they can talk to you about. But keep in mind, you still only want to post photos you look good in.

So, for example if you've been travelling, post a photo of yourself in a different country. If you enjoy the gym, post a gym selfie. If you have a cute dog (always a winner) post a photo of you with your cute furry friend.

What this does is it gives the other person conversational topics that they can talk to you about. For example, if you have a photo of yourself under the Eifel Tower in France and they've been to France themselves, they will have a conversation starter already there for them to ask you if you enjoyed France too. If you have a selfie at the gym and they also enjoy the gym, they will find that attractive and they can talk to you a little bit about the gym.

Your photos should make it easier for that person to be able to start a conversation with you. Also, you'll enjoy the conversation more because it will be about something you'll both be interested in.

Your Dating Profile Bio

The bio on your dating app is very important to men

who are looking for a relationship. Men who just want sex won't care about your bio. But men who genuinely are looking for a long-term partner will. They will want to only match with people who they would find attractive AND interesting. And sometimes if they aren't 100% sure on your pictures, the bio can tip the scales in your favour and get them attracted to you and get you that match with them.

Ok, so what should you put in your dating profile bio?

It's super easy once you know what to put! First of all, you need to put what you are looking for. If you are looking for a relationship, put that!

Don't be aggressive by saying things such as, 'No to guys just wanting me for sex, I will not respond.' It will make you come across as a little hostile. Instead, simply say, 'Looking to find that special connection with someone.' It's a much softer approach but still delivers the same message that you want someone long term.

After that, sprinkle in your personality, such as, your likes, hobbies, what you do for a living, your interests etc. It will let the person see what you're about and if they have any similar interests as you.

Then after, you always want to give that person an easy conversation starter to have with you. You could put something like, 'Give me your best joke and I'll rate it out of 10' or 'Tell me 3 cool facts about yourself'. Experiment with lines of this nature and you'll be surprised at how many people will appreciate this and use this as an opening line to start a conversation with you.

Avoid saying anything negative in your profile, such as listing things you hate. Positivity is attractive, negativity isn't. Also, if you start writing negative comments, people will think you are hard work and people will not want to talk to you.

The goal of your bio is to make yourself appear as an approachable, positive person who people want to talk to, whilst giving them easy conversation starters to use to start talking to you.

An example of a good bio is:

'Looking to find that special connection with someone <3 Ok, so a little bit about me... I'm a lawyer by day, but by night I'm a sporty girl who loves the gym! When I'm not in the gym, I do have an artistic flare about me and love drawing and painting. I'm definitely the best cook you'll ever meet (well I think so)! I also love watching comedies! I personally think I'm hilarious, but you'll have to see for yourself... Tell me your best joke and I'll rate it out of 10!'

1. This bio says a bit about who this person is, but not too much, so the other person will have to ask some questions to find out more.

2. It shows this is a confident person.

3. It gives them an opener to use by asking them to tell their best joke.

4. Also, the bio isn't too long and won't bore the other person. Keep it short, sweet, and engaging to keep their attention.

Experiment with your bio, have fun and show your personality!

How to move it past the Dating Apps

So, you've met someone on a dating app, and you think you'd like to get to know this person a bit more because they have a good vibe about them. Fantastic! You will then need to get the conversation off the dating app...

You have two options... Get their phone number or social media page (Instagram is best). The reason why I say you need to get the conversation on to Instagram is because it's the perfect chance to have a little look on their page and see what they are really about. And if your social media page has good pictures of you and it shows off your personality, they will find you more attractive.

So, when the conversation has been going back and forth for around 10 messages or so, say to them, 'What's your Instagram? I'll message you on there as I hate talking on this app!' Simple. 9/10 times they will give you their social media. If they don't, that's ok and they will suggest their phone number instead.

When they give you their Instagram, message them on there saying 'Hi' or continue the conversation on from the dating app. Like I said, you'll be able to showcase who you are much better on there. Also, it gives them the opportunity to show interest on your pictures and posts by liking or commenting on your posts, so you will definitely know if they are interested in you or not. Because if they like what they see on your social media, they will start displaying more interest to you.

How to go from meeting someone online to real life

There is definitely a way that makes you and the other person feel more comfortable when you've met someone new online and you want to move it forward to meeting them in real life. Also, this way will reduce the chances of you getting ghosted because of someone getting nervous to meet you. People can get a little overwhelmed and anxious if you just met them online and then straight away ask them to meet you in real life.

Instead do this... This process should take about 3-7 days for it to be effective...

So, you first meet them online, let's say a dating app, then you have a good conversation, and you get their phone number or social media page (Instagram is best for this). So, this is where it begins...

1. Exchange texts as normal.

2. Send them voice notes to get them used to the sound of your voice.

(Do these first two steps for a few days, and if they vibe is good, then move onto the next stage) ...

3. Say to them, 'Can I call you instead? It will be good to talk on the phone with you instead of texting'. If they agree, then great. If they don't, they may be nervous. If this is the case, don't make a big deal about it and say, 'No problem' and then you MUST let them suggest talking on the phone with you when they are ready, otherwise you'll be coming across as pushy and it will be unattractive.

But we are assuming they will say yes. Then have a conversation on the phone, and if all goes great, then onto the next stage…

4. Suggest to them, next time that you talk, it would be nice to do a video call. I always think this is very important for yourself too because even though phone calls are good, when you are on a video call, you will get a feeling for that person's vibe and if you'll get on with them or not. If all is going well on the video call, do this next...

5. When the energy is at a high point and you're both having fun, suggest to them it would be nice to meet up and then say to them, 'I have to go' and then say, 'Drop me a text when you're free to meet'. Then leave the conversation…

6. If all has gone well, they will text you and let you know when they can see you. And then you can arrange a date with them to meet in real life.

This whole process always works to make people feel comfortable with you because you are slowly introducing different elements of yourself to them by progressing the interactions from texts to phone conversations, to video calls, to meeting in real life, and they won't feel as nervous about meeting you because you've escalated the interactions in a steadily progressive way. Also, when you go and meet them in real life, it will feel like you already know each other.

Social Media and Dating and Relationships

Like it or not, social media is something that is very hard to avoid when dating in the modern world. Social media really is what you make of it. It can be used incorrectly, or it can be used to massively enhance your dating life. If you know what you're looking for on social media you can tell A LOT about a person, sometimes for better or worse. You can avoid the wrong guys, you can make some amazing connections with people that you would have never met in your day-to-day life, you can make yourself seen to potential people you may end up dating, and much more. Never underestimate the power of social media.

In this chapter I'm going to be giving you a few tips to enhance your dating life and some things on what to look out for and avoid. Anyway, let's dive straight into it...

Show a glimpse of who

you are to the world

Your social media is a perfect chance for you to show the world a little bit of who you are. What you look like, your interests, your thoughts, humour and much more. I'm not saying that you need to become someone who overshares their whole life story online, but showing a brief glimpse into who you are is a great thing. Think about it... You match with someone on a dating app, you start chatting and you think to yourself, 'I really like this person'... Most people will then have a quick search for them on social media to see what else this person is about. And if you like what you see, it only makes you more interested in that person.

You can make your social media present you in the best way possible for other people who want to view your page. Men will always search on social media for who they are chatting to on the dating apps. When they do this, you want to show them interesting and cool things about yourself. And if you have pictures that you look great in, post them on there too! It will give them more things to talk about with you...

For example, let's say you're really into a specific sport and they see it on your page and they think it's cool; it will give him an easy conversation starter to have with you and get the conversation flowing.

But it's not just from dating apps that you'll meet new people on social media! Other people on that social media platform may come across your page and think, 'They look cool, interesting, attractive etc, I'll add her'. Then you will both have the opportunity to start a conversation with each other if they start following your page.

But if your social media doesn't have anything about yourself on it (or a very limited amount), then you'll get overlooked by someone you could have been a great potential match with.

The less you make yourself seen, the harder it is to be found.

I'm not saying that you need to be an influencer, or even post much, but giving a glimpse of who you are on social media will do great things for your love life. Trust me...

How to slide into their DM's (messages)

Lots of people get nervous to message people first on social media. But there's no need to be. Follow this easy path and it will feel natural to message people on social media.

Ok, let's take a social media platform like Instagram, and you see someone you like the look of... I want you do this...

First of all, if you already follow each other, that's great. But, if you start to follow them and they don't follow you back straight away, don't worry too much, as you still may have a chance with them, and they may follow you a little later on. So, follow them and do this...

1. Like or comment on a couple of their pictures (a couple of the newer ones, not the very old pictures or you'll look a bit stalkerish). Now the bait has been set, I want you to wait...

2. Wait and see if they like or comment on a post of yours

in return. If they do that's great because they are showing interest back to you...

3. If they upload a new post, like or comment on it. Keep posting on your own page every so often as well and see if they continue to like or comment on your posts too. If they do, everything is looking very good!

4. Then I want you to do this if they haven't already messaged you... When they like or comment on another post of yours (I would say after you have liked or commented on about 3 posts on each other's pages), message them saying, 'Are you going to say hello, or are you just going to like my pictures?' It's really that simple.

If they are attracted to you, they are sure to appreciate this as they may have just been a little nervous about starting a conversation with you. You'll get a positive response 99% of the time because you both have clearly shown interest in each other.

Once you have exchanged messages and got the ball rolling, you'll realise just how easy it is to slide into their DMs and start a conversation. Try it out and see for yourself!

What do I do if my partner refuses to put me on his social media?

As a Dating Coach I get asked this question a lot. You can tell a lot about a person's intentions in a relationship by whether they are willing to post you on their social media or not. In my opinion the only couple exceptions to this are if that person uses their social media exclusively for work, or if they hardly ever post anything at all to their social media.

If your partner is constantly posting things about their life and sharing their experiences with the world whilst they are in a relationship with you, yet they never post you, or refuse to post you on their page (for example: a picture together), it's a huge red flag.

What are they hiding you for? Or who are they hiding you from? People will refuse to post you on their page because they want to appear single, or they want people to approach them because people won't know if they have a partner or not. Be very cautious of this red flag because in all of my time as a Dating Coach I have seen this many times; and every time it turns out that the person who hides the fact that they have a partner is ALWAYS up to no good or has unfaithful intentions.

I'm not saying that they must post pictures of you both together all of the time. But, for example, if you have taken lots of pictures on a day out together and they post pictures of the day on their social media apart from the pictures with you in it, then that's very suspicious to me.

Like I said, there are exceptions to this, but not many. Don't be hidden away. Confront your partner about this. Hear out their excuses, and if they don't have valid reasons, then keep your eye out for other suspicious behaviours. Your partner should be proud to be with you and have nothing to hide!

Does it matter if they like another woman's picture on social media?

It all depends on the circumstances of who's picture it is and why they are liking it, and this segment applies to you if you are exclusively dating him.

You can tell a lot about the mindset of a man who is exclusively dating someone and how he acts on social media.

So, there are times where it is ok for him to like other woman's pictures... These times are when he is genuinely friends with the woman AND the post that he likes is not a thirst trap (a thirst trap is when someone post a seductive post in hopes to get flirtatious or sexual attention). If a friend of his, who is a woman, posts a nice picture of herself on a day out or if she posts something funny or inspiring, then that's not disrespecting your relationship if he likes it. But if his friend posts thirst traps and he likes or comments on it, then it is disrespectful to the relationship.

If he starts liking some a random woman's selfies or thirst traps, then that's a huge red flag in my opinion. I've never seen one case where the man turns out to be a good boyfriend when he has this mindset. It always comes to light further down the line that he's been up to no good. Confront him about it if this happens to you and ask why he thinks that is ok. If he gets defensive, then there's a reason why. It's because he feels caught out.

The honest loyal men I've met in my life who treat their partners with love and respect, don't go around liking other women's thirst traps. I'm not saying that if he scrolls through his social media and sees a woman that he doesn't know that he can't look at her picture. I'm simply saying there's no need to press that like button. It's one small step from liking a picture to dropping them a message. Trust me on this one!

Texting

Texting can be confusing for many people in the world of dating. Many people find themselves asking: When do I text someone? How long should I wait between texts? How can I tell if they like me over text? There are many questions that people want the answer to when texting someone that they like. Luckily, I have those answers! Texting is something in the modern dating world that you must get good at and learn to understand, otherwise you can lose out on a potential great connection that you could have had with somebody...

A little patience goes a long way

Do not worry if they haven't text you back for a little while! Now when I say a little while, I mean a few hours, or if they are genuinely busy at work etc. Or sometimes some people like time to themselves and take a while to respond and that's ok as long as they communicate that.

But the golden rule is, when that person does eventually text you back, DO NOT instantly text that person back if they made you wait a long time for their reply (unless they have a good reason). You'll be coming across as needy and completely in their frame. You need to have patience with this.

You know that feeling you get when you've sent a text and you are waiting for them to respond, and then they do, well, it's exciting isn't it! You want to recreate that feeling for them when they receive a text from you.

So, if they made you wait a few hours for their reply, do the same back! Once you start doing this, they will become more excited by your texts if you don't instantly reply to them, and because of this they will be the one who will be eventually replying to your texts very quickly!

A little patience and fighting those urges will pay off big time!

Save the deeper conversations for the night-time

Get into the deeper conversations when texting them at night! This is surprisingly effective to get somebody to truly open up about themselves.

We all have psychological filters that make us a bit more reserved in what we say. However, at night when we become a bit more tired, our psychological filters become weaker, and we are a lot less likely to filter what we say. Also, people aren't as busy at night, so they are more likely to give you their attention and a flowing conversation is much easier to create.

Ask them deeper questions about themself at night to get a more honest and in-depth answer. This will form a deeper connection between you both, making you both feel like you've known each other for a long time. Think about it... The deepest conversations are always late at night!

The cliff hanger technique

The cliff hanger technique! So, you know your favourite TV series always ends an episode on a cliff hanger and it makes you excited for the next episode? Yeah, well, you can do this over texts with someone as well.

All I want you to do is this... When the conversation is at a high point and it's flowing, fun or even flirtatious, then that's when you tell the person 'Goodnight' or that you have to get back to work etc.

People always remember how you last made them feel. And if the last emotion they had with you was a fun, positive one, then they will be excited to talk to you again.

Also, when you are the one ending the conversation, you control the frame, and the frame is that they will feel like they are the one chasing you, which will make them want you more. Simple, yet effective.

Who should text first?

Ah, this age-old question. Ok, so most of the time it doesn't really matter who texts who first. However, there are some things to keep in mind about this...

You don't want to be the person ALWAYS texting first. It should be 50/50. If you text them first one day, let them text first the next day, otherwise you'll appear needy if you always text them first each day, and that's not very attractive. Let them chase you a little bit too.

However, I want you to follow this one rule about who texts who first... If you've been on a date with a man, you MUST wait for him to text you first after a first date! This is more important than you may think because a gentleman who has been raised correctly will text a woman first after the first date regardless of how the date went.

Firstly, he should make sure that you got home safely. Secondly, he should tell you that he had a nice time (assuming the date went well) because a gentleman won't want to leave a woman confused about whether he likes her or not. And thirdly, it's just good etiquette. If he doesn't text you after the first date, move on and know you can do better because you don't want a man who can't even do these basics anyway.

DO NOT DOUBLE TEXT!

Double texting is when you send someone a message, and if they take a while to reply and haven't responded to you yet, you send another message.

I know you may get an urge and start thinking to yourself, 'If I send them another text then maybe they will get a notification, see it, then respond to me'. Don't do this! The instant you double text someone is the instant you become needy. People will get a sense of desperation from you, and I guarantee they will lose attraction for you. Instead, be patient, wait for them to respond and you'll get a much better reply. Fight your urges!

Don't text each other too much or too little

You want to leave a little bit of mystery, but you don't want to appear avoidant either. You want to find that nice balance. You don't need to be texting them 24/7, because when you meet in person, you will run out of things to talk about.

On the other hand, if you text them every few days, the other person will start to think that you're not interested in them or don't have the time to date, which will result in them not pursuing you any further.

The easiest thing to do with this is only text them when you're genuinely not busy. If you're busy with friends and family, or working, or at the gym, or doing whatever you enjoy spending your time doing, then don't text them. They will be more excited to receive a text from you and you'll be coming across as somebody who has other things going on in their life, which is attractive. When you get the nice balance of texting someone not too much or not too little, you will know it!

Avoid one-word replies!

I cannot say this enough... If you send a one-word reply

and don't get a response or left on read, it's because the other person will either assume that you don't like them, or they will assume you want them to carry the conversation. Because of this you will end up getting left on read and could miss out on a potential great connection.

So, whenever you're texting somebody just add something onto the text that they can respond too. This could be a question, continuing on from something that they have said, adding value to something they have said, or starting a new topic of conversation that they will find interesting.

If you're struggling to come up with a reply, take your time and reply to them a little later when you're in a more talkative mood. Whatever you say, as long as it adds value to the conversation, it's better than one-word replies.

First Date Tips

The first date can be a very nerve-racking experience for many people, but it doesn't need to be. People panic about what they should wear, what to talk about, who pays on the date and many other things! But there's no need to worry yourself, once you know what to do on a first date everything will be plain sailing and you'll enjoy those first dates because you won't be panicking about what to say or do! Ok, let's get into the tips for your first date...

Who pays for the first date?

It is an important moment when the bill comes for the first date! You can tell A LOT about a person from they handle it. Don't underestimate this moment. I believe a man should be chivalrous and pay for the first date, BUT whether he should see her again entirely depends upon what she does too.

So, first of all, this is what not to do as a woman when the bill comes on the first date... Do NOT just sit there and say nothing and expect him to pay for the first date. When the bill comes you should say one of two things...

The first one, when the bill comes, is to say, 'I'm happy to go halves on this if you like.'

If he says 'No' and he insists that he pays, then say to him,

'Are you sure?', and if he's been raised correctly, he will say,

'Of course, I will get this.' Then after he has paid say,

'Thank you', and if you enjoyed his company and still want to hang out with him, say to him,

'I know this cute bar, I'll get you a drink.'

He will LOVE this. You are showing him you are a team player but also allowing him to be chivalrous by letting him get the bill on the first date. It works every single time.

Another option you have, if you are someone who prefers to pay for themselves when the bill comes, is to say,

'Let's go halves on this, I always pay my own way and I won't take no for an answer.'

Say this in a nice way... not aggressively. This will show him you are a team player. It also lets you see if he respects it when you say that you WANT to pay for your own half. Lots of people prefer to pay for themselves and their date must respect that.

But, no matter what, don't just sit there and EXPECT him to pay. That's a quick way to not getting a second date. Lots of men will be seeing if you're a team player or not. But, like I said, a gentleman will always be prepared to pay for the whole bill on the first date… He just wants to see if you expect him too.

But, if a man goes on a first date with you and is EXPECTING you to go halves on the bill, then that's a red flag right there! It shows he doesn't have good social etiquette.

Where to go for a first date

Choosing where to go for a first date is important. You want to go somewhere that feels relaxing, quiet, but not too quiet, and somewhere where you can get to know that person. The goal for the first date is to see whether you want to see that person for a second date. Nothing more, nothing less. If you start thinking this person needs to be someone that you're going to spend the rest of your life with, then you will be putting too much pressure on that date and yourself. So, the only goal for the first date is getting to know them well enough to see if you want to go on a second date with them or not.

So, where to go... First of all, and I can't tell you this enough… go somewhere public! The world is full of scary individuals, so make sure you are somewhere where other people are in case they end up being a weirdo!

A lot of people think going for a meal on the first date is a good idea. I strongly disagree. It feels like an interview and a very high-pressure situation for you both. Also, if you don't like them, it's very rude to make an excuse and leave halfway through the meal. So, I suggest something as simple as a coffee date. It's public, quiet but not too quiet, and it's a very relaxed environment. Plus, you can be there as long as you like. If it's not going great, then you only have to endure the time it takes to drink a coffee and then you can leave. If it's going very well, then you can have another coffee. Simple. You'll be able to have a better flow of conversation too, because it won't feel formal and like an interview.

If you still want the date to carry on after the coffee date, suggest going for a walk after. You'll be going to different locations which will strengthen the familiarity between you both as well. Then you could even go for a snack to eat after. That's a great first date!

This first date suggestion works for everyone I have recommended it to, because it's a low-pressure environment where people feel relaxed, and that will make the conversation flow much easier. This works equally well for going to a quiet bar at night for a drink. Just don't get drunk though or you're opening up a whole other world of potential problems. Keep the drinking light and don't get drunk, so you don't make any mistakes you could up end regretting!

Should I wait for him to ask me on the first date?

This is a question that I frequently get asked. The answer comes down to some simple psychology and analysis of who you're talking too. The main principal that really matters is about how much interest they are giving you in the talking stage. One important thing that you want to remember is to not ask them too soon or you'll come across as a little needy, but don't take too long because you'll appear as someone who isn't interested.

I say the right time to talk about going for a first date is around 3 days into the talking stage, assuming everything is going well.

I know a lot of women like the man to ask, and to other women it doesn't matter who asks who. But, if they ask you first then great, but if they haven't asked by the 3rd day of getting to know each other in the talking stage, then this is what I want you to do...

If they are giving you a good amount of interest (consistent texting, phone calls, compliments etc), then it is a good thing to ask them to go on a first date with you, if that's what you want to do. You're basically rewarding their positive behaviour towards you by asking them for a date.

A man will love the confidence you are displaying by asking him on a date, as many women will wait for the man to ask them on a date. If a man has a lot of women interested in him, but they all have the mindset of waiting for him to ask them on a date, and then you come along and you are the only one who is confident enough to ask him on a date, you will stand out massively to him. It shows you aren't intimidated and made nervous by him. BUT only ask him if he has shown you clear interest by positive, consistent behaviours towards you.

There is one thing to keep in mind though... If you ask him and he says he is busy etc, you must NOT ask him again. He must be the one who asks you the next time, otherwise you are falling into his frame, and you will appear needy and desperate if you keep asking him. But if you ask him when he is showing you interest, it is very unlikely that he will say no to you.

So, if he hasn't asked you yet, ask him out and display to him that you're a woman who goes and gets what she wants. And lucky for him... it is him! He just may not have asked because he really likes you and is trying to think of the right way to ask you because he's scared of messing it up.

And one last thing that will give you that extra bit of confidence to ask him out on a date is... If you don't ask him, someone else will and you will be there knowing that the man you want is on a date with someone else, and you missed your opportunity.

First Date conversations

Navigating the conversation on a first date can be a bit tricky for many people. But go into it with a positive attitude and see it as an exciting opportunity to see if you and that person vibe well together.

The things that you want to avoid talking about on a first date are: Your exes, religion, politics and negative or controversial topics.

The main goal of conversation on a first date is to have yourself come across as someone who is relaxing, interesting, curious, and fun.

The way to make yourself come across as relaxing is to avoid the heavy topics such as the list of things I said NOT to talk about. (If someone asks you about politics or religion, by all means talk about it, but don't push your opinion onto them).

Also, don't be too loud. On a first date, you don't want the whole room staring at you because your being over the top. It's not attractive or relaxing.

And lastly, take your time and never seem in a rush when you are talking.

The way to seem interesting is to talk about things that you have done, wish to do and are planning to do with your life. Just make sure that you don't brag about your life too much and wait for all of these things to come up naturally in a conversation.

An easy way of doing this for example is like this...Let's say you have been around the world travelling during your life, which is a very cool thing to talk about that can lead to many other conversational topics; you can then ask them where their favourite places they have been are, and their number one place they wish to go and why etc. Naturally, they will talk about it and if they have good manners, they should ask the same back to you. Then when you talk about yourself travelling around the world, it won't appear as bragging, it will seem like it naturally come into the conversation, and you'll seem like an interesting person which is attractive.

Sidenote: It's then very easy to link this to other topics of conversation. For example, if you have been to France, you could then say you love the food there and why. Then because you are talking about food, you could then ask them what their favourite food and favourite restaurants are etc. This is super easy with some practice and the conversations you can have are limitless.

The third trait that you want to display when having a conversation on a first date is that you are someone who is curious. When I say curious, I mean someone who is inquisitive and loves getting to know people and different things. In a world where many people care mostly about themselves, someone who has an outward curiosity towards others and learning new things is very attractive. Also, people who are curious are great listeners which is always very desirable in a partner.

And lastly, it is important that you come across as somebody who is fun! People are going on first dates because they want to meet someone who they find attractive, and they can have fun with.

Joke around with your date, tease them a little, be flirty. All of this will get their heart racing and it will be very attractive. If you're asking, 'How do I be flirty?', then there are many ways to flirt in this book which will get them thinking you're the best first date they ever had!

Don't get drunk!

Many people drink on a date to calm their nerves. Please do not get drunk! It will be a complete waste of your time if you get drunk on a date. You won't be able to be your best self and will ruin your chances with someone who could have made an amazing partner for you.

Also, you won't be able to able to recognise any red flags they are putting out there, or you won't be able to recognise any green flags. Also, you may end up having sex with a man on the first date and then he will compartmentalise you into the category of women who are just an easy person to get sex from when he is horny.

Trust me there is no benefit to getting drunk on a first

date. If you do drink, please limit yourself to the point before you start feeling tipsy. You want to be 100% aware of what you and the other person is saying and doing.

How to Get into a Relationship

There is a correct way of getting into a relationship, and there is a wrong way. It's all about setting the correct foundations of what type of relationship you want it to be. And hopefully you want a relationship that has strong foundations built upon mutual respect and getting to know each other the correct way whilst keeping everything exciting. It's all about balance. Not to take things too fast, and not taking things too slow.

It's about how you say things at the right times too. You will have windows of opportunity to escalate things forward, and you need to be able to recognise them.

Every relationship can be different, but what I will teach you in this chapter is the healthiest way to build a lasting relationship... I will start from the first date and give advice all the way up until you end up in a relationship...

What should the first date be like

if I'm looking for a relationship?

You want to get things off to a good start when building the foundations of a healthy relationship. This makes the first date very important. The first date should be something casual and relaxed. Your only goal on a first date is to see if you want to see each other again for a second date.

On the first date you do NOT have sex with him. The most you should do on a first date is a kiss. Not a heavy make out, but a smooch is fine. You must not let the man think he is going to get sex from you on a first date. If he pushes for sex on a first date, he has no interest in a relationship with you. He only wants sex. If he says he is looking for a relationship, but also makes the conversation sexual on a first date, then he is lying to you about wanting a relationship! Don't fall for this classic trap. He's giving you false hope of a relationship in order to get sex from you.

For the location of a first date, I recommend a coffee shop date, a drink at a cool bar, a nice walk, or anything that is casual and relaxed. Also, don't make the first date too long, a few hours maximum. You always want to leave them wanting more.

The conversation on the first date should be kept positive and casual. Nothing too heavy. You're just here to see if both of your energies match with each other, and if you find them attractive.

If all goes well on the first date, make sure that you WAIT for him to text you first after the date. If he does text first and is telling you that he had a nice time etc, ask him when he's free again (if he hasn't already asked you) so you can organise a second date with each other.

The 2nd date

It's great that you're on a second date because I'm assuming the first date went very well! Now you want to keep that energy moving in the same direction. The second date can be made into something that's a little more traditionally expected of a date. This is because you've got to know each other a bit on the first date, so you will both be at ease a little bit more with each other for the second date.

So, I recommend that you either go for a dinner date, a classic dating activity (such as mini golf), or something a little more adventurous and active that is something you both enjoy. Just something more than meeting for a coffee. That will set the standard that you are on a proper date together, so they will know that you are pursuing a romantic relationship.

The conversation can move onto topics that are a little deeper than what you would have had on the first date. However, don't make it too personal and fully expose everything about yourself, but you can expose a little more about yourself compared to the first date if you feel like you can trust them, and they are doing the same. Just don't reveal too much about yourself such as your address or personal details like this because you don't fully know this person yet. If all goes well, fantastic! At the end of the night give them a smooch if that's what you both want to do.

However, you still must NOT have sex with them. It's

still too soon. If they are pushing for sex, then they don't want a relationship. The first date was merely a formality for them. They always planned on having sex with you on the second date. So, don't see them again.

But, if all goes well, then you can text them first after the date letting them know you had a nice time and then arrange the third date.

The 3rd date

The third date is the MOST important date. For a lot of people, it's the tipping point of whether you will go forward into seeing that person exclusively (not seeing other people), or not seeing each other again. So, if you like them, you will want to do this date the right way.

The third date is a date where it won't damage your chances of having a relationship with them if you have sex with them. With that in mind, if you both have good sexual chemistry with each other, you want to make everything seem as natural and effortless as possible when you do go to have sex.

You want to be in a location where it seems natural to have sex (Only if you want to have sex). I recommend when you are arranging the third date with each other that you invite them over to your home, or go to their home. Then say to them that you'd love to cook for them, or order food to eat in. This will make everything feel much more intimate between you both instead of going out and being surrounded by the public. This way you can both be a lot more private, and if things to go well and escalate sexually, you can act in the moment. Also, sharing food with each other is a psychological trigger that will make people feel closer, and that is why I recommend this.

The conversation on the third date can become deeper, but do not have the exclusivity talk this early on until you have had sex. If you start saying that you don't want to see anyone else before you have sex with them, then you will appear that you are using sex as a reward for their commitment, and that is a bad thing. So anyway... As the night goes on and all goes well, and if you do have sex, then great!

Even though you have had sex, do not let them stay overnight at your house, or do not stay overnight at theirs. It's too soon. Say that you have to be up early for work, or to see friends/family etc. Then after they leave, or you have left theirs, you must WAIT for the man to text first. A man who is a gentleman will always text first after the first time you have had sex. If he does, then great. If he doesn't then don't pursue him (It's rare that they won't text first after having sex for the first time when it's the third date because he should be emotionally invested in you by this point). But if he does text first, that's great.

Then in between arranging the fourth date with each other, you need to have the exclusivity talk. This is the conversation that is make or break for whether you move forward into a potential relationship or not. You must be very clear with how you say this to them. Say it like this...

Say to them that you don't want to date anybody else because you are enjoying dating them... Then you MUST say that you aren't saying that you want to be their girlfriend YET, but you want to start seeing each other, and not date other people, and see how it goes.

9/10 times they will say 'yes'. If they start seeming undecided about it and don't say yes to this, or they say no to this, then do NOT continue dating this person. They will be dating multiple people at the same time, and you are only an 'option' to them. And if they are having sex with you but don't want to even see how things go, then they will never settle down. Trust me on this. But if all goes well and they want to start seeing you exclusively then that is fantastic news, and then it's on to the next phase...

After the 3rd date

So, you have both agreed to start seeing each other, meeting regularly, having sex and all the other things that come along with seeing someone... Now is the time to start transitioning it into a relationship. If all is going well, it should happen within at least two months after the third date. It's actually super simple to transition from dating exclusively to being boyfriend and girlfriend...

During this period of time where you are just seeing each other, to transition it into an official relationship, all you have to do is keep everything fun and enjoyable like you did when you first met. That's all there is to it. Remember, how you get them is how you keep them. They liked you for how you were when they first started dating you. So, you don't have to have a big sudden change of character because you want to shift the relationship into something more serious.

Lots of people start becoming more serious in their

behaviours and planning too far ahead and it can scare some people away. But, if you just keep it fun and enjoyable in this stage of the relationship (it should be like that 99% of the time throughout the relationship in life, sprinkled in with serious parts when needed), then you will have them wanting to be with you in a long-term relationship. So, if all is going well and you love spending time together, and it's been about two months, and you want to be officially in a relationship with them, it's easily done...

All you have to do is say to them something similar to this... 'I was thinking, we've been dating for a while, and it's been going amazing... I would like to be boyfriend and girlfriend if that's something you'd like to do as well?' If all has been going great, they will 9/10 times agree to this. Then congratulations to you, you are in a relationship!

If they say no, ask them why. Don't get mad at them, just see what they are thinking. If it has been 2 months, and they say they aren't dating others but want to see how things still go, then give them another month maximum. But if it has been 3 months, they are dating you regularly, having sex with you regularly and other things of this nature, then something is definitely not right if they don't want to be officially boyfriend and girlfriend. Question them as to why they are holding back because there aren't any valid reasons why they should be holding back on getting into a relationship with you.

I believe their main reason is because they won't be wanting to commit, because they will be wanting boyfriend privileges without the full commitment. And that is NOT ok! These types of guys always have one foot out of the door, and if this is the case, pull away from them because it's rare that they will change their mind.

But hopefully all will go well, and this won't be an issue. I'm just letting you know in case this does happen. But, like I said, if you have done everything right, 9/10 times you will get the result that you want!

How long should you wait in between dates

Knowing how long to wait in between dates is something that you will need to know. You don't want to rush things because you'll be coming across as needy, but you don't want to wait too long either because you are going to lose the momentum that you have built with that person. You want to find a nice balance where you're becoming a part of each other's lives, but you aren't smothering them.

You need to think of your interactions as energy... If you give them too much energy too fast and it becomes highly charged very quickly, then it will more than likely be over before you know it. It will be very difficult to maintain momentum at very fast pace.

If you start off seeing each other too much, then you'll run out of things to talk about, you won't be as excited to see each other because there is no waiting in between dates, and you won't be enjoying your normal day to day life as much and neglecting the things that they liked you for.

On the other hand, if you wait too long in between dates, then you won't be able to establish a connection with that person because their brain will see you more as a stranger who they occasionally date instead of a potential partner. You won't be invested enough in each other's lives, and it will always fizzle out when this is the case.

The trick is finding the right balance. In the early stages of dating someone, I believe you should be seeing each other at least once a week. Preferably two. For example, once on a Wednesday and then see them again on that Saturday night. But once a week is enough in the very early stages. Two times is better, but it's not the end of the world if you can't. But when you see someone once a week, you will start becoming someone who is regularly in their life.

Once you are both dating each other exclusively, you should be seeing each other twice a week at least. Three times is great (it doesn't have to be long, even having dinner together at home is a date). This way you will start forming a bond with each other. Then once you are both girlfriend and boyfriend, see them as much as you both like.

Why you shouldn't have sex with someone too soon

This is a common mistake people make. Getting caught up in the moment and then having sex with someone who they haven't taken the time to get to know.

I say that you should wait until at least the third date to have sex with someone. If you do it sooner, then it rarely ends good for you.

Lots of men will compartmentalise women into

categories. They will have women who they see as someone who is easy to get sex from, and women who he sees as potential girlfriends. They might like having sex with you, but if you give men sex too quickly then they will see you as someone who they call when they are horny. But, if you make them wait, they will see you as a woman who they see as a potential partner because they will have more respect for you.

However, if you make a man wait too long for sex, he will see you as a tease and will start questioning if you have ulterior motives, or he will think he is in the friend zone and then stop dating you.

The key is not giving him sex too early, and not making him wait too long. Ultimately the choice is yours, and you have sex whenever you are comfortable. But, just to let you know, this is how most men think...

Make him emotionally invested in you before you have sex

One of the goals when dating to find a relationship is to make someone emotionally invest in you. When someone emotionally invests in you, they will want to commit to you. But, if you have sex with someone too soon, they will be less likely to be emotionally invested in you and this is when ghosting can occur, because they will either categorize you as someone who is easy sex for them when they are horny and they won't fully respect you; or they will feel like they've got what they want and then ghost you.

So, this is why you should take your time when dating.

This is a game of chess not checkers. Resist those sexual urges for a better result at the end of it all. Therefore, you should have these dates with him and take a while getting to know him.

Ask him questions, make him feel like you're the person that he can confide his thoughts and emotions with, become the person who he is excited to see, share fun experiences with each other, become his friend first (but a friend that he has sexually chemistry with of course). Once you do this, he won't want to lose you. You'll become a part of his life and he won't want that to change.

Think of it like this, people become attached to things that they put their time and energy into; and if he puts his time and energy into you, he won't want to let you go. Also, emotions are stronger than people's logic. If you can make him feel an emotion towards you, which will happen naturally when you spend time together, he will form an emotional attachment to you, and that is a strong bond that he won't want to lose.

Don't date multiple people if you really like someone

A common thing that is said in the dating world is that you should be dating multiple people at the same time. I say it really depends on the situation. So, this is the way I want you to manage different people you are interested in or talking to when dating...

When you are only in the talking phase with people, you can talk to as many different people as you want. There is no limit here. You have no connections or ties with anyone, so do as you please.

So, you may be asking, 'What do I do if I have been on a first date with someone and I really like them?' If this is the case, I want you to do this...

Because it's still very early days with this person, carry on talking to different people at the same time. But, if you have a second date lined up with this person, do NOT go on any other dates. And whatever you do, do NOT have sex with anyone else. If you both feel like you have shared a connection, and then you date others or have sex with other people, then eventually they will find out (most of the time) and it can really ruin the excitement and hopes that person has for you.

Think of it like this... For example, you have both been dating and in a relationship for a few months and then they find out you have had sex with someone else whilst you two were dating... Well, that will only end badly. 9/10 times they will be hurt by this, and it won't make the connection you both shared feel as special to them. Let's say they were having sex and dating others after you two had an amazing first date. How would that make you feel? Not very good I imagine.

You should only be talking to others to keep your options open until the 3rd date. But, if you've had 3 amazing dates and have a good connection, stop talking to others and stop searching for a romantic connection with other people because it will not serve you in any way. You have already got what you are looking for. This will make the dating experience you both shared feel very clean, special and uncomplicated with no issues arising in the future.

How to be More Confident when Dating

Having good confidence is a must have if you want to make yourself as attractive as possible. Your confidence can get people finding you so attractive that they won't stop thinking about you.

A woman who goes and gets what she wants is very attractive to a man of high value.

If you're not a confident person, have no fear. I have some tips for you to try and practice, and in no time, you'll be feeling so confident that it shines through, and people will say it's one of the most attractive things about you. Let's get into it...

Slow down

Slowing everything down is one of the easiest ways to make yourself appear more confident. People who are nervous tend to talk very fast because they just want to get talking over and done with. They also tend to have fast body movements and can be jittery in their movements. This is because they have nervous energy and their body's jittery movements are an outlet for that nervous energy. So, if you feel like this is you and you feel like this happens a lot when you are talking to someone you find attractive, I want you to try this...

When you go into any conversations that you have with friends or family etc, be aware of how you're coming across. Slow down the way you talk and make your body movements more relaxed and slower. Once you start getting into the habit of doing this with people that you aren't attracted to, it will be much easier to do it when you are talking to someone that you find attractive because you've made it a practiced habit.

If you feel like those nerves are bubbling up when talking to someone that you find attractive, take a deep breath, compose yourself and SLOW EVERYTHING DOWN... When you do slow everything down your date will think you are someone who has everything under control, it will put them at ease around you, and you'll come across much more confident and attractive.

Get yourself into a talkative state

This is one of the most powerful tips for building confidence. I have done a lot of public speaking in my life and, for me, getting into a talkative state really helps with my confidence before I had to do something that made me feel nervous. So, before you talk to your crush or someone you're about to go on a date with, I want you to do this...

Let's say you're going on a date this evening; I want you want talk to and have conversations with as many people in your life that you possibly can that day. This can be family, friends, co-workers, the cashier at the shop, whoever really. But what this does is it gets you into a talkative state, so you won't get into your head throughout the day and overthink everything that you're going to say on the date. Also, it gets you into a flow state, where everything will come out of your mouth much more naturally. This really helps with any nerves you may have.

I've had to talk in front of big crowds before, so what I would do is go around before the event and talk to everybody and anybody. It definitely worked for me, and it will work for you too. Even though you are going to only be speaking to one person, the same practices that I have done with public speaking will work for you in your dating scenario too. Everyone I have recommended this tip to has said it's a very simple tip, but a complete game changer for them when it comes to helping them overcome their nerves for their dates.

Practice, Practice, Practice

If you're somebody who struggles with confidence, you need to remember that every confident person you have ever met in your life started in the exact same place you have with their own confidence at some point. The only real difference between you and them is your life experiences. Confidence comes from practice.

The most confident daters in the world are people who have been on many dates and seen what's worked for them and what doesn't work for them. Then they learn from their mistakes and move forward feeling much more confident in themselves because they have the knowledge of what does work and what doesn't work for them.

These days, many people put so much pressure on themselves to never fail at anything. We get scolded in school for not doing well on a test and this trickles over into our adult life and it's not healthy. Everyone will make mistakes at some point. So, what I am saying is, put yourself out there, practice, and don't be scared of making mistakes, because that is how you learn!

If someone asks you for a date and you think it could go somewhere, then go on that date. Even if you're nervous, go. Have the mindset of thinking of it like 'training' for when the person of your dreams comes along. If the date goes well, GREAT! If it doesn't, that's ok. Recognise why it didn't go well, learn from the mistakes, and make sure that you do your best to not repeat these mistakes again in the future.

Confidence comes with practice, and if you keep putting yourself out there to practice dating and talking to different people, your confidence will be at an all-time high. Then when the person of your dreams comes along, you'll be able to put your best self forward, and I have no doubt they will love being on a date with someone who comes across so confident.

Remember, the first steps of anything that you do are always the hardest, but when you look back in time, you'll be amazed at how far you've really come with your own confidence!

Body Language of a confident person

People can tell if someone is confident by their body language. You can really dominate a room by how you position your body. It will also make you 10 times more attractive! So, in this section I'm going to give you a few tips on how to come across as someone who is much more confident in themselves when you are talking to people. Also, when you do these body languages, you will be tricking your brain into thinking that you are confident, so you will feel more confident anyway. Think of it as a sort of placebo effect. Anyway, let's get into it...

1. Stand up tall, put your shoulders back and don't look down.

This one is simple. People who are nervous slouch forward into themselves to make themselves appear smaller so they can hide from the world. Confident people always stand up tall because they want to make themselves seen and it looks much more powerful when you are stood upright. Have those shoulders back, with your chest forward to show that you command the room. Also, nervous people always look at the floor. This is because they are trying to avoid eye contact because they find it unsettling. Confident people always look people in the eye when they are talking to them.

2. Make your body language relaxed and take up space when sitting down.

When you're sat down talking to someone, you want to make yourself look as relaxed as possible. Lean back in your chair. Put your arms and legs in a relaxed position that takes up space. You can still cross your legs, but perhaps lean them to the side a little if it feels natural to do so, because it takes up more space. You can appear very confident by the way that you're sat, and it can be very attractive!

3. Walk with a purpose.

You can walk into a room and give off a confident energy by the way that you walk into it. If you walk into a room looking lost and unsure, it's doesn't look confident or attractive. Walk like you always have somewhere to be. Even if you don't, fake it. You'll look like a person who is in control and that's far more attractive than someone who isn't.

The way that you talk

There are a few things you can do by the way that you talk to make yourself appear more confident. I'm going to give you a few tips for you to follow, and once you get good at this, you'll recognise people who are confident will also do these things when they are talking...

1. Stop using 'ummms' and 'ahhhs' when you are thinking about what to say to someone.

Saying 'ummm' adds nothing to the conversation and makes you appear unconfident because you are unsure of what you want to say, and clearly just saying 'ummm' to fill the silence.

2. Make statements more than you ask questions.

If you keep asking a lot of questions all the time, you will appear unconfident because you will always be in that person's frame. You will also look unsure of yourself, and it will appear as though you are uncomfortable talking about yourself. Instead make statements more than you ask questions. A good example of this is, instead of saying, 'Do you like the decoration in this room?', you could say, 'I love the decoration in this room'. The first one is a question you are wanting an answer to and therefore in their frame. The second one is a statement, and you are expressing your opinion. And if the other person is socially capable, they will add onto your statement. Just don't forget to ask questions here and there. Just be aware that statements are more powerful for displaying confidence. However, too many statements and no questions at all, will make you come across as self-centred. Get the balance right and you'll come across as confident but also curious about them, and they will love that!

3. Use your pauses.

Adding pauses when you are speaking is a huge display of confidence. Don't fear having a brief bit of silence when you are talking. If you say something that has an impact, pause, and let it really sink in. Too many people say something that's of high worth, then continue talking and then they lose out on a great chance to make more of an impact with what they are saying. This is because nervous people just want to say what they have to say and get it over and done with. Whereas confident people don't shy away from having that silence after they have spoken because they are confident and comfortable within themselves to not have to fill the silence with pointless conversation. Pausing also allows the other person to contribute to the conversation without interrupting you, and they will appreciate that.

The mindset of a confident person

The mindset of a confident person is an intriguing topic. Many people are confident because of different things. The main thing that fuels confidence is practice and experience. However, there are some ways that you can change the way you think to feel more confident when you don't have experience and practice to fall back on, so when you go into a situation that you aren't feeling experienced in, you will still feel more confident than most people.

I naturally have a nervous personality and I must put myself in check when I feel nerves bubbling up. Some people are more naturally inclined to be nervous than others. It's just their nature. So, how I got over my naturally nervous personality is by adopting this mindset... There are two things that really worked for me...

1. Learn to let go of all expectations and outcomes.

For example, if you are nervous about a date, it's likely that you are nervous because you have an outcome that you desire in your mind, such as, you want them to like you or you want that person to be everything you hoped they will be. This will already put pressure on yourself and the date and will give you a lot more nervous energy. So, let go of all expectations. If that person is meant to be for you, it will happen. They will like you for you and you will like them for them. The worst thing that happens is that you don't like each other, and that's ok. Best thing that can happen is that you live happily ever after.

2. This mindset really helped me the most when I felt nervous in my life… I want you to think of the situation you're going into, let's say a date for example. I want you to identify how you're feeling. Let's say you are nervous. Now, I want you to think of the deepest, darkest day of your life. For many of us, it's a close family relative passing, or it could be something else that has happened to you. Then I want you to think about how that time made you feel. Terrible, I expect. Now I want you to compare that dark day to the date you are about to go on… It doesn't seem that scary after all does it? A date cannot compare to the worst day of your life. You overcame that day, and this date is something that is nothing to fear, but to enjoy instead.

For myself, I was very ill for a very long time where I thought I was going to die. So, whenever I'm nervous, I think and know that whatever I'm going into doesn't scare me because I've been through much, much worse. It's got me through some tough scenarios. Use those negative experiences to your advantage and you will be the most confident person in the room. I promise you this works from my own personal experience.

The Spotlight effect

Ah the Spotlight effect. We have all fallen victim to this. We think that everyone around us can see every slightest move we make, judging us, thinking about us, and why we are doing things.

Well, most of the time this isn't true at all! The person you are talking to is a lot less focused on you and a lot more focused on themselves than you may realise. They are having the exact same thoughts you are having. 'Do they like me?' 'How am I coming across to them?' 'Does my hair look good?' and many more thoughts just like these!

So, when you are talking to someone and you start having these thoughts about yourself in your head, I want you to pause and think, 'This person is thinking about how they come across to me, not how I come across to them'.

This will take a lot of pressure off yourself. The goal is to be conscious of what you are doing to make yourself come across as attractive and confident as you can, but at the same time, not over thinking about yourself so you become stuck in your own head and very nervous. Having a healthy amount of self-awareness of how you come across is key.

Once you develop this mindset, you will relieve a lot of pressure off yourself, and you'll see that nearly everyone is stuck in their own heads and mainly focusing on themselves.

Your Appearance

In the world of dating, looks do matter. I don't care what anyone says, you will not want to start a sexual relationship with someone you don't find physically attractive. You might meet the nicest person ever, who has a great personality, but if you think that person isn't sexy, I guarantee that 99% of the time you will see them as a friend instead of someone that you want to start a sexual relationship with.

The world of dating is a very competitive one, and you need to look your best if you want to attract the type of people that you want. Otherwise, women who do put the work into looking their best will get more attention from men, even if their personality isn't as good as yours.

In this section I'm going to give you some tips that will help you attract the type of men that you want. I will also add that none of these tips are expensive! Looking your best doesn't need to cost you a fortune. All you need is a keen eye for what looks good! Let's get into it...

Hair

When you are putting together your look, your hair is a huge part of whether you will look attractive or not!

All men, whether they are conscious of it or not, will look at a woman's hair, and it can massively impact if that man thinks you are attractive or not. Evolutionary speaking, our brains are evolved in a way that we judge how healthy someone is by their hair. Whether it's thick, full, long etc. This would determine whether a man found a woman attractive or not, because he would think that she is healthy if her hair looked healthy. And the healthier a woman looked to a man, the better chances that the babies he has with her would be healthy too, ensuring their survival back in the caveman days.

Now, because of science we know this isn't always the case, and hair doesn't mean everything in regards to someone's healthiness. But men's brains will still look at a woman's hair to determine if she is healthy or not; and then if men's brains thinks a woman's hair looks healthy, they will consider that woman more attractive. You can use this piece of evolutionary psychology to your advantage.

Make your hair look as healthy as possible. You want to style it in a way that makes your hair look fashionable and healthy. If you feel like your hair isn't healthy, do not worry! This is where a great hairdresser can make it look amazing for you! They can style it with different things, such as extensions to make it look fuller, add colour to it, style it fashionably, tell you the best products to make your hair look it's best, and much more!

Either way, when you are dating, make sure your hair looks the best it can look, and I 100% guarantee that men's eyes will be drawn towards you much more!

What should I wear to make myself as attractive as possible?

We've all been there... Getting ready for a date and panicking about what we should wear. 'Will they like this?' 'Does it make me look hot?' 'Does this make my figure look good?' We can all relate to this. But to make yourself more attractive with your clothes is quite simple. Just follow these basic rules and you'll do great...

Follow the fashion

This one may seem obvious but many of us get stuck in our ways and don't try out the new fashions. With your fashion, you need to be more flexible. When you follow the fashion, it's a high value trait to have. This is because it shows that you are socially aware and socially intelligent because you recognise the fashion trends within your society.

I want you to be honest with yourself... When you are sat down talking to someone and you are stuck in your old fashion ways, and they look good in new fashionable clothes, you can't help but think they look great and fashion forward.

So, don't be shy, break out of your box and try something new!

One thing I will also add to this is fashionable clothes do NOT need to be expensive! You can be fashionable with cheaper clothes! You can buy the most expensive designer clothes, but if they don't look good, then there's nothing the label can do about that. But on the other hand, you can buy some cheaper clothes that look very hot and very fashionable. Don't get suckered in by the brand name, it means nothing. People won't be sitting on a date with you thinking, oh she's wearing this brand, she's hot. They will only carc about what it looks like.

Accessorise

Accessorising is an important part of your outfit. Don't overdo it though, otherwise you'll look like you're trying too hard. Instead, wear some nice subtle earrings, a nice necklace that can really compliment your outfit, and a couple of finger rings always look good too.

Accessories make you look fashionable, but they also do something else... They give the person an opportunity to compliment you. For example, if you have a nice necklace, they will tell you how much they love it. Then it gives you a chance to return the compliment. Everyone is a winner!

Wear good fitting clothes

Sometimes you see people wearing super expensive clothes, but if they aren't a good fit for that person's body, it can look terrible. You want to wear clothes that compliment your body.

If you have a good figure, wear clothes that show off your figure. It's that easy. You want to leave some things to the imagination, but at other times, you want to flaunt what you got. Trust me, all men love it when a woman wears good fitting clothes that show off her figure.

Peacocking

This is a term that many of us have heard before, but if you haven't, peacocking is where you wear something that will make you stand out. Peacocking is a high value behaviour because it shows confidence, and if you look back throughout human history, it shows a higher social value.

Throughout the history of human society, we have learnt to recognise and associate people who stand out in a crowd (because they look good and fashionable) as people who are often considered high value.

So, when you are on a date with someone, or even in your day-to-day life, wear something that makes people's eyes drawn towards you. A good example of this is a nice coat that makes you stand out. Or simply a stunning dress.

The goal is to have people's eyes drawn towards you because you look good, and your fashion choices stand out in a good way. Peacocking done the correct way will do amazing things for your love life and result in having more people feeling attracted to you!

Cosmetics

When I say cosmetics, I'm talking about things like

having your nails done, wearing make-up that suits you, having a good skincare routine etc. These small little details, when added up together, can really make a big difference to how good you look!

Dress to impress who you WANT to impress

You can use your own style of fashion to your advantage when dating, if done correctly. Dress to impress who you want to impress. See your style as you marketing yourself. The goal is for your fashion choices to give you more opportunities in the dating world.

So, for example, let's say you love dressing in fashionable athleisure clothes; then chances are you're going to be attracting men who like women who go to the gym.

Let's say you like to dress fashionable, but quirky and eccentric; then the majority of men you are going to attract will more than likely be confident, quirky types of men.

Another example is if you love wearing fashionable business wear; then guys who are in the business world will take more notice of you because of the way you dress in the office.

The reason this works is quite simple. Our brains are still hard wired from evolution to think like we are in a tribe. And we are going to find people who we have more in common with (because they seem similar to us) more attractive. This is because we can see them fitting into our 'tribe' much easier. We will also believe we have more in common with people who dress like us.

So, if you want to attract a certain type of man, be aware of the style of fashion you choose to wear because it will have a big impact on the type of man who will find you attractive.

Make sure you are wearing sexy lingerie

When you're getting ready for a date, you need to look good underneath your outfit too. Let's just put it like this... Those who fail to prepare, prepare to fail. Let's say you have been on a great date... You go home and things get hot and sexy... you strip down to your underwear... and you're wearing some very unsexy underwear... Now that is a turn off for you and for him!

You need to make sure you are wearing some sexy lingerie when you are on a date in case you end up having sex! Sexy lingerie will turn him on even more, and it will make you look so much classier.

Also, when you are on a date and you know that you are wearing sexy lingerie underneath, it will give you a confidence boost! Even though you are the only person who knows what you got on underneath, it will still make you feel 10X sexier...

2 Outfits that will make you look HOT on your Date

Do you have a date planned but you just don't know what to wear? Well, no need to panic. I have two PERFECT outfits for you to wear on your date that is guaranteed to make him more attracted to you. I have given you an outfit to wear on a day-time date, and an outfit for you to wear on a night-time date...

Day-time outfit

On a date during the day, you want to wear an outfit that's casual but not too casual. You want to show off your figure, but at the same time not look like you are trying too hard. The key is having an outfit that gives off a feminine energy. Feminine energy is very attractive to men and it's easy to give off feminine energy by the way that you dress.

Here's your Day-time Date outfit:

- Knee knee-high boots

Every man LOVES knee knee-high boots. They are very feminine and very sexy. For the daytime I recommend wearing a more casual knee-high boot with a low heel.

- Tight well fitted jeans

Wearing tight well fitted jeans is always a good look. This will show off your curves. Tight well fitted jeans combined with the knee-high boots with a heel will emphasis your booty and it will look HOT. At the end of the day, he is a man. He's going to glance at your booty when he gets the chance. May as well make your booty look as good as possible.

For colour I recommend a lighter colour as this will highlight your curves more than a darker colour would.

- <u>A tight well fitted top</u>

A top well fitted top will show off your figure and look great. Now the key to making this outfit look good is to tuck the top into the jeans. This way it will really emphasis all of your curves. It's a very feminine style and he will find it very attractive.

- <u>A cute belt</u>

I highly recommend wearing a cute belt to go with this look. It will tie the look together very nicely.

- <u>White nail polish</u>

White nail polish just looks good! It's feminine and classy. Always a winner.

- <u>Jewellery</u>

Wear some jewellery but not too much. A couple of rings, a nice feminine watch always looks good with this outfit, and some subtle earrings too (don't wear massive earrings as not many men find them attractive). The key to wearing jewellery is to not overdo it. Subtle but classy feminine jewellery is what you should be aiming for.

Night-time outfit

When you are picking your outfit for a night-time date you need to aim for a classy feminine look with an edge of sexiness to it. This is easily done...

- Knee-high boots with a heel, or high heel shoes

Knee-high boots and high heel shoes are both very feminine. They both add a classy and sexy feel to the outfit. My personal favourite are the knee-high boots, but a nice pair of high heel shoes also look great.

- A black dress that shows off your figure

Honestly, you can't go wrong with a well fitted black dress. However, you need the dress to be the right length. Don't wear a dress that's too long, it's not sexy. But on the other hand, don't wear a dress that's too short. You want to wear a mid-length black dress that shows some leg. Men love a dress with the slit showing some upper thigh. This looks great and gives off a classy and sexy vibe.

White or Red nail polish

White and Red nail polish always look great. White nail polish looks a tad classier, but red can look a little sexier. Both are great. I personally think white looks better, but red is also a good look.

- White gold jewellery

White gold jewellery looks very classy with this look. If

you don't have any white gold jewellery, then no need to worry. Stick to the light colours of jewellery and avoid the yellow golds and colours that are too bold.

Subtlety is key to making your jewellery look good with this outfit. You don't want to overdo the jewellery. Just wear enough where it adds to the outfit but doesn't overpower it.

I suggest wearing a couple of rings, a nice feminine watch or bracelet, a loose necklace, and some nice earrings.

These are two outfit suggestions that I know will make you look classy and sexy. Whatever you wear on your dates is your choice; but for those who aren't too sure of what to wear, I guarantee that men love the way a woman looks when she wears these two outfits.

The Art of Good Conversation

Having good conversational skills is an absolute must when dating! Have you ever spoken to someone who's words are just so captivating that you don't want to stop talking to them? Well, you can have these skills too. You need to view having conversations as a form of art. You need to know when to push, when to pull, when to be expressive, how to engage your audience, and much more.

The art of conversation is something that will take a little bit of practice, but once you get good at it, it will change your life for the better. Having good conversational skills can make you so much more attractive as well. You could be a 10/10 with your looks, but if your conversational skills aren't good, you won't have much of a chance of getting those 2nd or 3rd dates. Good looks will only get you so far when dating. But, if your conversational skills are good, you can make almost anyone attracted to you! Also, it's not just good for dating, it's good in all aspects of your life! Anyway, let's get into the tips that will make you a master at the art of conversation....

Be expressive

I had a friend growing up who was the absolute best storyteller I knew. He could tell me something as mundane as a story about him buying bread down the shop, and it was genuinely captivating to listen to. So, I asked him, 'How did you get so good at telling stories?' and the answer is simple. He was expressive with the way he talked. He changed the pitch of his voice to match the story. The highs, and the lows. He laughed when something was funny. He acted surprised when telling something that was surprising in the story. He was expressive with his face when talking. He was always very expressive with his body language. He used big hand movements to suck you into the story. And he also used well placed pauses when talking to add suspense to the story when he was telling it. He would get to the good juicy part of a story and say,

'You would never believe what happened next.' Then I would be on the edge of my seat like,

'What?' Then he would say something like,

'Honestly you won't believe me, it's crazy.' Then I'd say,

'Tell me!' because I was dying to know. Then he would carry on the story and continue to be expressive with his body language and tonalities whilst delivering the juicy parts of the story. He built suspense the correct way when telling his story and that was exciting.

These are simple things that everyone can do. Practice

being expressive when talking, and people will be on the edge of their seats listening to what you have to say!

Bring the conversation back to something that relates to them

Bringing the topic of conversation back to something that relates to the person you're talking to is an easy way to keep that person engaged in the conversation. People love talking about themselves and things that relate to them.

I want you to do a little social experiment for yourself. This may ruin a lot of interactions you have with people because you'll realise what people really want to talk about... 99% of the time it's things that relate back to themselves!

I want you to have a conversation with someone and wait to see how long it takes for that person to make the conversation about them. You could talk about any idea, or any topic, and they will somehow make it about themselves. It can be very frustrating when you see this happen because it happens in almost all conversations. But if you use this to your advantage and you make the topic of conversation something that relates back to them, you will appear as if you are someone who is very easy to talk to, and they will enjoy the conversation with you so much more.

This is interesting though, because when you see this happen a lot, you'll be a lot more conscious of people who DON'T have this trait. And those are the types of people you can have deep, intellectual conversations with because these types of people who don't talk about themselves as much are a lot more interesting to talk to, and they are much better company. And they are rarer than you may think. These are the types of people who will make better partners for you because they will actually listen to you and respond to what you are saying, therefore having much better conversations with you.

Always leave them wanting more

Having a good conversation with someone is fantastic. But you need to learn the art of when to leave the conversation.

Have you ever spoken to someone you've had a good conversation with, and you have had a good impression of this person, and then the conversation starts to slow down, and then talking to them just becomes a bit tedious? Whereas if they left the conversation 10 minutes earlier, you'd be excited to talk to them again? Well, I'm sure like many people, you have! This is where you need to learn when to leave the conversation so you leave the best impression of yourself that you possibly can.

The fundamental rule of this is to always leave them wanting more. This is easily done. When you are talking to someone, ALWAYS leave the conversation when it's at a high point. Never when the energy is dipping. Leave when you feel the conversation is at the best it's going to be, and the other person seems very engaged in what you are saying. This will make them very excited to talk to you again. This is called the 'Cliff hanger' technique. Think of your favourite TV series. They always end the episode on a cliff hanger, and it makes you excited for the next episode. View your conversations in the same way and watch how people crave talking to you again!

Don't interrupt!

This tip is simple. Don't interrupt someone when they are talking. It's one of the most frustrating things in the world. People like to have their contributions to the conversation listened to. When they are interrupted, they will feel disrespected in the conversation.

All you need to do is sit back, relax, and let that person finish what they are saying, and they will appreciate it. This tip may sound basic, but have you ever been on a date with somebody who won't let you get a word in because they kept interrupting you? I expect the answer is yes, and it is super annoying.

Don't interrupt people in conversations and you're already better than 50% of people out there at communicating.

Great conversation starters

Sometimes finding things to talk about can be tough. But have no fear, I'm going to give you some great conversation starters to use that will get the deep conversations flowing. These work for in person conversations, when you are on the phone, and when you are texting somebody. Use them whenever feels right to you! Here they are...

1. What did you first notice about me?
2. If you met yourself 10 years ago, what advice would

you give to yourself?
3. What's one thing you've wanted to say to me but haven't yet?
4. Do you think we knew each other in a past life?
5. What would you want to be famous for? And if you don't want to be famous, why?
6. When is a time you've been the hero to someone, and the villain to someone else in the same story?
7. What's a quote that you've heard that's had the biggest impact on you and why?
8. When's a time you've changed someone's life?
9. Are you chasing your dreams? Or are you scared to chase them in case you fail?
10. What would you say your real life 'superpower' is?
11. If you were in a room with everyone you ever knew, alive or dead, who would you go to first?
12. Do you believe in soul mates?
13. What was the biggest thing that surprised you about me?
14. If you only had 6 months to live, what would you do?
15. Where's the number one place in the world you would want to travel to?
16. If you had to be locked in a room for 7 days with someone, who would it be and why?
17. If you could change 3 things about your life, what would they be and why?
18. If you could go back in time and change something in your life, what would it be and why?
19. When you were a kid what did you say you wanted to be when you grow up?
20. What was the single biggest moment that changed your life?

Remember the small details

This is a simple tip, yet one that always gets overlooked... Remember the small details!

Let's say a man is talking to 2 different women... One of these women doesn't remember the small, intimate details about his life. And the other woman pays close attention to what the man is saying and remembers all of the small details about his life.

Now when the man is speaking to either one of these women, who do you think he will feel more of a connection with?

It's going to be the woman who pays close attention to the little things in his life that matter to him. For example, this could be his mother's name, his birthday, his dog's name, his favourite sports team, what his hobbies are, what him and his friends do for fun together... and many other examples just like these.

When you talk to him during a conversation and you remember these little details about his life, he will feel like you have been closely listening to him, and it will make him enjoy talking to you so much more.

If you are someone who listens to him and knows the small intimate details of his life that matter to him, then he will feel much closer to you compared to somebody who only remembers the surface level topics of his life.

So, when you are talking to him make sure that you subtly drop in these small details into the conversation. For example, you could say, "Are you seeing you mother,

Stacey, later?" This may not sound like much, but just by using his mother's name, you have shown him that you care and listen to the small details in his life that matter to him.

This will make him feel more familiar with you and will accelerate him feeling a connection with you.

Long-Distance Relationships

Long distance relationships are becoming much more common than they used to be. Especially with the growing number of remote workers these days. And I think it's a brilliant thing. People are now meeting people who they never would have met before because of the internet and the accessibility to remote working that's available.

People are now dating people who they never would have dated before; and a long-distance relationship won't be long distance forever. If two people are in a long-distance relationship and it goes well, they will move in together.

Lots of people are closed off to the idea of a long-distance relationship because they think it can be very hard work. If you follow the rules that I'm going to give you, you will find long-distance relationships so much easier, and you will find that they can be very rewarding.

Let's say you meet the person of your dreams, and

you get on amazingly well with them. They have good morals, you find them attractive, and you have amazing conversations with them... Are you really going to let that slip away because a little bit of travelling is involved? You'd be crazy to miss out on the opportunity of starting a relationship with them because of that!

Think of it like this... Yes, you may have to travel a little now, but in a year or so time, you could be living together, get married and live happily ever after; OR you can continue to date people in your area who you have no connection with. I know which one I would rather pick, and I think you'd be crazy not to pick someone because a little bit of travelling is involved to be with the person you want to be with.

Anyway, if you are looking to get into a long-distance relationship, or you are already in one, I am going to give you some tips to make everything much easier and enjoyable for yourself and your partner...

Have a date planned for when you are going to see each other next

Having a date planned for when you are going to see each other next is super important when in a long-distance relationship. It makes everything so much easier because you have something to look forward to. I want you to think of it like this...

If I told you to run but I didn't tell you how long you have to run for, you will get tired very quickly because not knowing will have a big mental strain on you. But if I said to you, 'I want you to run for a mile', it will be much easier for you mentally. This is because you will have a distance in your mind and you will know exactly how long you have left, letting your mind to be at ease.

It's the same when in a long-distance relationship. If you don't know when you are going to see your partner again, it is incredibly frustrating. It will make the wait seem like forever! But, for example, if you know you are going to see them in a week, I 100% guarantee you that you will manage your emotions much better. This is because you will have a 'finish line' in your mind... It's the not knowing that's the hard part.

You will both need to be organised and want to put the effort in for this to work. But think of it like this... You will get to travel and be with someone who you love to be around. It's a win-win. Think of it as having two homes. A little vacation away from your normal day to day life for you and them. Put it into a positive frame like this and you'll really start seeing the benefits that a long-distance relationship can offer you.

Trust and maturity

Having trust in your long-distance partner is the MOST important thing when in a long-distance relationship. If there isn't 100% trust between you both, then there is no point being in the relationship. When you can't see that person every day, they could very easily hide a secret life from you, and that's why trust is so important. When getting to know someone who's a long distance away from you, don't ignore any red flags or inconsistencies in their stories or behaviours. You need to trust your instincts, and if you have a strange feeling about something or someone, don't ignore it. But if you trust them 100%, and they've never given you a reason not to, that's great!

Also, the maturity of both of you is extremely important when you are in a relationship with someone who is a long distance away. You will both need to be very understanding about each other's time and schedules.

Don't panic if they haven't text you back for a few hours. They could be out with friends, working, or many other things. If you start pestering them and over questioning them about everything, you will come across as controlling. But if you trust them 100%, you won't feel the need to do that. Trust and maturity go hand in hand.

Also, be understanding if your partner gets frustrated that they can't see you sooner. They may get agitated, but don't take it personally (unless they are being nasty to you). Let them be frustrated for 5 minutes if they need to be, as long as they aren't directing it at you. If they are a bit quiet on a call, it could be because they miss you so much. But if you assume it's something that you have done wrong and start getting defensive, it will push them away. Always be kind and calm with each other when the other person is frustrated, and you'll have a much stronger relationship.

Communication is Key

Communication in a long-distance relationship is EVERYTHING! If you have a breakdown in communication with your long-distance partner, it can be the end of the relationship. Consistency and consideration make a healthy long-distance relationship.

I suggest regular phone calls. Once every couple of days minimum. Video calls are much better because it's the next best thing that you can have with someone instead of actually being with them in real life. Everyone has time to do this at some point over the course of a couple of days. For example, when you are cooking your dinner, put your phone on the side and have a conversation with them. Instead of watching a show on TV, give them a call. These are just a couple of very simple examples. When you both do this, it shows you are both wanting to make time and effort for each other.

I also believe video calls are much better than normal texts. You can't really express yourself properly over a text, and texting can become quite dull. Whereas a video call with someone who you have great conversations with is never boring.

Consistency in communication is very important too. Just because you are a long distance away from each other, it doesn't mean you should go a week without talking to each other. It could make one of you anxious about how the other person is feeling when there is a breakdown in communication. This will make someone anxious because they are unsure of where the relationship is heading.

Try and have a video call at least once every couple of days. This will reduce a lot of anxiety in the relationship!

Plan the dates in advance

In a long-distance relationship one of the biggest

challenges is battling the frustration of being apart. But this can be made much easier by having something exciting to look forward to.

Planning your dates ahead with your partner is fun and exciting and will make the wait of seeing each other so much easier. When you plan ahead you will find that you actually end up having better, more exciting, more adventurous dates than a lot of people you know who are in relationships with people in their local area. This is because you will truly value the time that you are spending with your partner, so you will want to make that time together as special and memorable as possible.

I've seen so many people in long-distance relationships who have the best times because they really make the most out of the time they spend together. For example, let's say you are planning a weekend away together, THAT'S VERY EXCITING! You know that when you see each other that you're going to have the best time because you will both truly cherish the time you have together!

So, plan those dates in advance and keep the excitement there for the both of you, and have something to look forward to when you aren't together.

And another great effect this has is because you plan these exciting dates at the start of the relationship, you are setting the foundations to what your relationship should be like in the future. You both know that you can do it and be adventurous, so you can always be planning fun dates just like you did when you first started dating!

Keep the flame alive

This is the biggest obstacle most people face when they are in a long-distance relationship. How to keep the flame alive! It can be tricky and frustrating to keep the flame alive... only IF you are dating the wrong person. If you're dating someone who you share an incredible connection with, keeping the flame alive isn't as hard as you may think it is. In fact, with the right person, it's actually very easy because you both won't want anyone else!

Keeping the flame alive consists of all the tips I have given you in this chapter. If you follow my advice when you are with the right person, everything will be heightened. The connection you share, the attraction you feel towards each other, the enjoyment of dates, the conversation, EVERYTHING!

Have a date organised of when you are going to see each other next, trust and understand each other, communicate, plan exciting future dates, and don't forget to FLIRT with them.

If you are in a sexual relationship with them, flirt and be sexual with them. You want them imagining what you two are going to get up to when you see each other next. This will make them want you so much more. It builds up the sexual tension in a good way, and it is an explosion of emotions when you see each other.

Do all of these things with your long-distance partner, and you'll be amazed at the results!

From the Dating Coaches Handbook

In this chapter there are many different flirting tips, ways of displaying higher value to build attraction, first date tips, and much more. The best thing about these tips is it will seem like you are doing nothing out of the ordinary, but yet, they will help you massively when you are dating. Let's get straight into the tips from the Dating Coach's handbook...

The False Time Constraint (FTC)

This tip is brilliant. A false time constraint is when you say to someone about yourself being restricted with time, and that you can't stay in their company for too long.

For example, you could be arranging a date with someone and say to them, 'Yes, I can go out for a drink tonight, but I can't stay out too late though as I have to be up early in the morning for work'. There are many different examples like this, but that's a common one you can use.

When you use a False time Constraint it does 3 things...

1. It will relieve anxiety for yourself and your date.

A FTC gives you an excuse to leave that date whenever you want. If you're not enjoying the date, you can simply say, 'It was lovely to meet you, however, like I said, I really do need to be up early in the morning, so I must go'. Knowing this, you'll go into the date feeling more relaxed because you know you can leave at any time you want to in a polite manner.

I always think of it as helping your anxiety like this... If I locked you in a room and I said to you, 'You can't leave until I tell you', you're going to feel nervous and uncomfortable. But, if I said, 'Go into this room and you can leave whenever you like', you'll feel completely at ease because you have the power. It's exactly the same when on a date. And because you will be more relaxed and feel more in control, you'll enjoy the date much more.

2. The second reason why FTC's are great is because it will make you look much less needy.

We all know neediness is not attractive, but when you are using a FTC you'll never look needy. So, when you use a FTC, when arranging a date for example, the other person will feel like you're not putting your whole life on hold for them. It will appear as though you are a busy person and you're going on a date to see if this person is a good match for you or not, instead of putting your life on hold because you're needing their company.

This will also make you appear as a high value person, and they will find you more attractive because of it. People find people who have more going on in their lives more attractive because being busy is a high value trait.

3. They will feel like they are chasing you.

Because you are the person who is effectively ending the date because you have used a FTC, they will feel like they are chasing you because you are the person who is being more elusive. When people feel like they are chasing you, they will automatically feel more attracted to you because you are coming from a place of higher value compared to them.

People love the chase, because every positive step they make from gaining attraction from you feels like a reward for them, so they will keep chasing you. It's positive reinforcement at its best.

Use those FTC's and you'll be shocked at how truly effective they are.

The Push-Pull technique (Flirting)

You may have heard of this flirting technique before, 'The Push-Pull technique'. It's where you give someone interest (the push) and then you give them disinterest (the pull).

The 'Push-Pull technique' builds attraction with someone because it will make the other person feel like they are chasing you. This is because you will be giving them flirtations and interest, but then you take it away from them so they will want to earn your interest again. When something has had something that makes them feel good and then you take it away from then, they will crave the thing that made them feel good even more. Plus, it's fun and playful when done correctly and can build a lot of sexual tension.

Also, as explained in the previous tip, when people feel like they are chasing you, they will automatically feel more attracted to you because you are coming from a place of higher value compared to them.

So, let's get into it... I will give you a few examples, and in your own time you can experiment with different ones and have fun with it. (All of these examples MUST be delivered in a fun, non-offensive and joking manner)

The 1st example: 'You're pretty hot for someone with no banter'

The push is the compliment, 'You're pretty hot'. The pull is the teasing, 'for someone with no banter'

The 2nd example: Give them a quick kiss, then lightly push them away and say to them, 'That's all you're going to get for now'.

The Push is the kiss. The pull is the light push away and saying, 'That's all you're going to get for now.'

The 3rd example: At the end of the date (if it went well) say to them, 'I actually had a really good time with you, it was a lot of fun. If you're lucky, and I'm in a good mood, I might see you again, but like I said, only if you're lucky'

You must make it very clear by your delivery and expression that you're joking and being flirtatious. It will then be well received. The push is the compliment, 'I actually had a really good time with you, it was a lot of fun'. The pull is the teasing, 'If you're lucky and I'm in a good mood I might see you again, but like I said, only if you're lucky'

The reason these are all effective for building attraction is because it spikes that person's emotions in a fun way. This makes the person feel like they are chasing you a bit, and as we all know, men love the chase!

The Perfume Tricks

Your perfume can be one of your best flirting tools when dating. Never underestimate it.

Ok, so I have a few tricks with your perfumes that you can do to make a man want you even more. Here's the first tip...

Perfume tip 1

First of all, before you go on a date make sure that you wear a nice perfume that you're certain he will like, then go on the date... Now, this is where it starts...

Assuming the date goes well, and you have a fun time together, I want you to do this... On your 2nd date I want you to wear the same perfume that you wore on the 1st date.

When you see him again and he gets a sense of smell from the perfume that you wore on the 1st date, it will trigger all of the emotions he had on the 1st date, which were good, positive emotions.

So, let's say you had a great 1st kiss, and he smells that same perfume that you were wearing during the kiss; he will get the emotions he had associated with the 1st kiss, which if it was good, will be positive emotions.

If all keeps going well on the dates and you're having a fun time, don't change the perfume. It will be on his clothes, in his car, on his pillow etc. Everywhere he goes he will get the positive emotions associated with you and your scent, and you'll be living in his head rent free. Simple, but it works amazingly well.

Perfume tip 2

The 2nd tip with perfume is, if all is going well with him, say to him, 'Do you like my perfume?' and if he says, 'Yes', say to him, 'Come here then..', and if you carry it around in your handbag, take it out and spray it once on his chest. Then say to him, 'Now, you can smell me all day long'.

If he's into you, he will absolutely love this, and you'll be on his mind all day because he will have the scent of your perfume right under his nose.

Only do this tip if he really likes you! But if he does really like you, this tip works amazingly well.

Perfume tip 3

This 3rd perfume tip will get him hot under the collar... Well, it's more about his perfume/aftershave really... Anyway, I want you to do this...

Say to him, 'I love the smell of your aftershave. Can I smell it?' Then instead of just leaning in to smell his aftershave, do this...

Lean in and gently put your hand on his chest, and at the same time, lightly grab his clothes and slowly pull him towards you. Smell the perfume on his neck then whisper into his ear, 'I love your scent', then gently push him away.

Doing it this way is so much hotter, and it uses the 'Push-Pull technique'. Trust me, he will love this! Give it a go and see for yourself!

How to compliment like a Pro

Who doesn't love a good compliment? Never underestimate the power of a well-timed compliment. It will do you so many favours! A good compliment can make someone's whole day. It can also turn the mood flirtatious.

In this section I'm going to give you 3 simple tips on how to compliment like a pro...

Tip 1: Use their name after you compliment them...

This one is simple, yet effective. Studies have shown that when we use the names of the people we are talking to, it builds familiarity and connection between us. For example, you could say to someone, 'You're so hot.' Or to add a little extra effect to the compliment, you could say, 'You're so hot, Adam.' It just sounds better. When we find someone attractive and they use our names when talking to us, it just sounds so good.

Tip 2: Don't compliment a hot person on their looks!

People who are considered generally attractive will always be complimented on their looks and it gets quite tiresome and boring to them. Instead, compliment them based upon their personality, such as their intelligence, ambition, energy etc. This will make it appear as if their looks aren't important to you because you genuinely like them for who they are as a person, and they will want to get to know you more because you're not like everybody else.

Tip 3: Look them in the eye whilst you compliment them!

So simple, yet it makes it so much hotter. Eye contact builds connection. Mix that in with the two tips that I've given you, and you'll have them melting in the palm of your hand!

The Power of Food

Never underestimate the power of food when it comes to building attraction. Remember, we are all animals and associations with food will forever be hardwired into our brain, and we will react to things and people in certain ways when food is involved.

When you are on a date with someone that you like, and you want to make a good impression, and you are eating together, I want you to do this...

Share some of your food with them! It's really that simple. If you are out having dinner, simply say, 'This tastes so good. Here try some.' Now, here is the important part... Don't just let them take food off your plate. Instead, pass it to them.

When you do this, something in their brain will click, and they will feel the positive emotions that they have with food will also be associated with you.

You'll always like someone who shares their food with you a lot more compared to someone who doesn't.

When you see the scene in the movies where people are sharing desert off their spoons with the person they are on a date with, yeah, well, it helps build attraction in real life too. It works equally well on men and women. Use our human biology and psychology to your own advantage!

The 3 Date Rule

Please, I urge you to listen to this bit of advice! The 3 Date Rule!

So, the 3 Date Rule is: You do NOT have sex with a man until AT LEAST the 3rd date.

Even if you have a lot of sexual tension between you both and the moment feels right with each other, I urge you to NOT have sex with him sooner than the 3rd date, and here's why...

Firstly, if you have sex with a man too soon, he's going to put you into a category; and that category is that of a woman who he can get quick sex from whenever he feels like it. And if you're looking for a relationship, it is very rare that it will work out the way that you want it too if you have sex with a man too soon because he won't see you as girlfriend material, instead just someone who will give him quick sex.

Secondly, there's a high chance that you will regret it! This is called BUYER'S REMORSE... Basically, your brain thinks that sex equals babies. Obviously, we have protection, and we know that when we have sex that it doesn't always mean that we will have children, but our brains still haven't changed from an evolutionary perspective and still thinks sex equals babies.

So, what will happen is after you have sex with him, your brain will assume that you may be pregnant with his child, but you didn't take the time to get to know him and find out if he is a high value man and if he would make a good partner for you, and a good father for your child. This is why that sinking feeling of regret happens when you have sex with a man too soon, and it's called 'Buyer's Remorse'.

And thirdly, if you make him wait to have sex until the 3rd date, then you will give him the time to emotionally invest in you to want to stick about after having sex with you, because he finds out that you're a great person who he wants to spend time with. I actually recommend in the BIG cities to wait until the 5th date to have sex because the big cities are notorious for men just wanting sex and nothing more, and jumping from woman to woman.

The men who want just a quick sexual encounter will fall to the wayside because they usually won't invest 3 dates into a woman, but the men who genuinely want to get to know you will continue to date you. Then when you do have sex with him after making him wait at least 3 dates for sex, he will be emotional invested enough to want to keep the relationship growing.

The Blueprint

One of our most powerful tools when dating is the ability

to listen. Most people love to talk about themselves and tend to lay out the map of exactly what they are looking for in a partner. All you have to do is listen and ask the right questions to find out what they want, and if they match up with what you're looking for, be sure to let them know (in a smooth way of course).

You should always ask someone what they are looking for in a partner. This is so they tell you what they want and, if you have any of those traits, subtly drop it into conversation that you have these traits.

For example, if they say they are dating because they want something long term, and you are as well, let them know about it. If they say that they want to find someone who likes doing adventurous things, and if you're adventurous, talk about the times you have displayed these qualities. If a life goal of theirs is to travel the world with the love of their life, and it's something you've always wanted to do, then say that's a goal that you've always had too.

When you do this, they will think that they've found someone who is perfect for them. All it takes is for you to listen to them and seeing if you want the same things. If you do, then it's much easier to build a connection with them...

'I feel like I've known you forever'

This tip is powerful. Very powerful, when you have done everything correctly.

Let's say that on your date you've had great

conversations, broken the touch barrier the correct way, shared a good first kiss, and had a fun time overall... I then want you to say this one simple little line... 'I feel like I've known you forever.'

This will have a powerful effect on the other person... If you feel like you have a connection with someone, point it out! It's rare to meet someone you click with. The best thing that could happen on a date is feeling like you've known them forever, and when you say this line, it will make it seem to the other person like you two were destined to meet, and perhaps you are!

I do believe there is that one special person out there for all of us. And when you feel like you click with someone, it's truly exciting! If they feel the same way, it will accelerate the attraction they feel for you immensely. HOWEVER, if you do say it and they feel the same way and all is going great, don't rush everything because you have clicked. Stick to the game plan and I promise you it will go smoother because you've said this one little line...

'What's your secret talent?'

When you are on date, I want you to say this to them, 'So, do you have any secret talents?' Chances are they will say yes and show you or tell you. Then 99% of the time they will ask you, 'So, what about you? Do you have any secret talents?' and if you do, now is the time to show them. But that's only part of it...

Show them or tell them your secret talent (showing them will have a much more positive effect as it's fun). Then afterwards say to them, 'I have many other secret talents, but only lucky people will get to see them…' It's fun, flirtatious and it gets them thinking about sex.

If you don't have any secret talents, I strongly suggest that you learn some as you can genuinely make some very memorable moments on dates when you do. It might sound silly, but if you don't have any secret talents, get on the internet, and learn some quick, for example, fun bar tricks. They are easy to learn and when done correctly can build attraction and make you stand out. I recommend the ones that involve you touching the other person to break the touch barrier in a fun, natural way.

So, overall, this tip will create fun moments, and it can also be made very flirtatious. Don't ignore this one as it can become one of your favourite tools to use when dating…

Location, Location, Location

Where you go on dates makes a huge difference. To really maximise building attraction with someone, you want to use where you're going for a date to your advantage.

A lot of people think going for a fancy dinner is a good first date. It's actually one of the worst ideas for a first date. There's so much pressure sitting across a table from someone you don't really know. It feels like an interview, which will make you both feel nervous. Also, if you're not really feeling any connection with your date, you will feel like you must endure the date until the end of the meal to avoid being rude, so you could end up being stuck in the company of someone you don't like for a couple of hours.

So, how do we use the location of a date to our

advantage? This is how... Our brains are calibrated in a way to not so much care about the specifics of a location (providing the location is safe), but it's calibrated to the NUMBER of locations we are with someone. If you can go to multiple locations on a first date then you will always have that person feeling much more relaxed and comfortable around you, which will help build attraction and familiarity between you both much faster.

So, what I suggest for a first date is this... Meet up for a drink (keep it simple). Then if you like that person and you are liking their vibe, suggest to them, 'Hey I know another great place to get a drink, you'll love it. Let's go.' Then proceed to go to the next location.

Whilst walking there you'll be more likely to feel more relaxed because the body language between you both is side by side to each other instead of directly facing each other, which won't trigger you or them feeling like you're in an interview scenario, so you'll feel more likely to open up to each other whilst you talk.

Then when you get to the new venue for a drink, again, you'll start feeling more at ease with this person and enjoying yourself more because you feel more familiar with each other.

Think about it; you meet at a venue, walk, have a drink at another venue, walk to the car or taxi to go home. That's 4 locations on one date. But if you just met them at the bar and went home straight after the date, there's no way you'd feel as comfortable around that person compared to if you changed the location multiple times during the date.

I tell my clients this tip all the time, and they are

surprised at how much faster the process of getting to feel comfortable around a new person is when you go to multiple locations on a date instead of just one location. Try it out and see for yourself!

We should really slow this down to speed it up

This is a bit of a strange tip that actually speeds everything up and makes somebody crave you even more. So, this is how it works...

It's all about setting the frame of the interaction so it makes them feel like they are chasing you, which will make that person feel more attracted to you.

I wouldn't recommend using this on the first date with the first kiss, but the last kiss on the second date is the perfect time to use it...

All I want you to do is this... When you are kissing somebody, very lightly push them away and say to them in a fun, flirty way, 'We should really slow this down.' Then go straight back in for another kiss, then be the first person to pull away from that kiss...

It will make that person crave you so much more! This is because people want what they can't have.

You go back in for the second kiss because it makes you seem like you're breaking your own rules. It will make the moment feel very hot and naughty to the other person. Also, when you do make out and kiss etc, it will make it more exciting for them because they feel like they are getting something that feels a little naughty to them.

Also, men LOVE the chase. It builds the right type of tension between you both, and makes it so you control the frame, which can make you appear more confident and attractive.

You only need to use this tip once for it to have a good effect. Give it a go and see for yourself and watch how it makes that person want you even more...

Lock in Props

This is a fantastic tip, so be sure to pay attention. A 'Lock in Prop' is an item that you give to someone to highly increase the likelihood of that person seeing you again, and it is a hot way to flirt with someone.

However, this can be done manipulatively if done the wrong way and for the wrong reasons. But if done the correct way and for the right reasons, it can flirtatious and hot.

So, first of all I'm going to teach you the wrong way of doing it to ensure that you don't do it this way, otherwise the other person will think you're manipulative and annoying...

So, here's an example of using a 'Lock in Prop' the wrong way... When a guy drives you home and you knowingly leave an item in his car, such as your coat, then you call him up saying that you've left something in his car, and can he drop it off to you, or can you come and pick it up from him.

A lot of people do this on purpose to 100% ensure that they see that person again even if they don't want to see you. It's super annoying, and if done repeatedly, it can be a real pain and they might start thinking you're just doing it as an excuse to see them again, and you will be coming across as desperate. Don't do this!

Now, this is the correct way of doing it... Don't do this on a first date, but perhaps a second or third date... Let's say you have been on an amazing date... When the mood is right, you've done something fun on the date, and then you are at the end of the date, perhaps after you've kissed, I want you to do this...

Let's say you have a ring, or a bracelet, (these two items work best, and they don't have to be expensive, they can just be cheap ones), these are going to be your 'Lock in props'. When the energy is at a high point, perhaps after the kiss goodbye, say to him, 'Give me your hand', then put your hand out.

9/10 times they will put their hand on top of yours. Then take off your ring or bracelet and put it on him. Then say, 'I want you to wear this tonight to remind you of me and then bring it to me the next time you see me.'. Then give him a quick kiss on the cheek, then leave.

Deliver this in a flirtatious way and you will have a very powerful effect on him.

There are three reasons why this works... Firstly, it will keep you in his head because every time he looks at the item, he will be reminded of you, which is great! Secondly, the subtext of the interaction is that you are marking your territory and that is very hot if you are both into each other. Thirdly, he is going to see you again because he has your item!

This takes confidence, but you will be greatly rewarded when you do this!

Setting the mood

Picture this... You're on a third date and you've invited them to come over to your place, and you're going to cook for them. Now, this can either be a super romantic evening or a complete disaster. We definitely want it to be a romantic evening! So, I want you to do this...

You need to create the perfect ambience. If this is the first time someone is coming to your home, it's a big deal! If they come in and the vibe doesn't feel right to them, then it can be a huge turn off.

I'm sure many of us will do this naturally, but first of all, make sure that your house is super clean! There's nothing more unattractive than walking into a dirty house.

Now that is out of the way, let's get into how to create the perfect ambience for a romantic date night in...

You want them to feel calm and relaxed when they walk in. So, my first recommendation is to make the house have a really nice scent. Lavender is a perfect scent for this scenario because it is a very calming and inviting aroma. Spray the room, the sofa, whatever you want. Just make sure the house smells nice. If you don't like lavender, use a different calming scent.

Secondly, the music. Now, in my opinion, it is very important that you play the right type of music. You must never underestimate this as it can really set the mood in the right way. You want something that is light, chilled, relaxing and sexy. In my opinion, I think that you can't go wrong with R'n'B on a date night. But that is my personal taste in music. You choose whatever music genre you like.

Just make sure it's got a chilled, relaxing tempo.

Thirdly, this may sound a bit basic, but it really does set the mood... Candles. Don't underestimate how good candles are at setting the right mood. There is something calming and romantic about fire. Dim the lights and light some candles. It is always a winner for setting the right mood.

Now I want you to imagine yourself walking into an environment like this. A clean house, candles lit, it smells nice, chilled, sexy music playing. It's impossible for someone to not love this. Try it out for a romantic date night at home and you never know where the night might take you...

Escalating the Touch

Many people get nervous at the thought of the first time that they touch somebody. They make it a big deal in their minds, and then often the first time people touch is when they kiss for the first time, and it feels like a big event that can feel quite unnatural for everyone involved.

Instead, I want you to practice escalating the touch. Escalating the touch is when you gradually build up the amount and type of touching that you do with someone so everything will feel very natural and easy. It can also make that person feel like they have known you for a very long time in a short amount of time.

So, in this section, I'm going to give you an example of how to escalate the touch with someone up to the point of the first kiss...

The first stages of escalating the touch should be things that are socially acceptable and under the radar. So, first of all, when you meet somebody, you want to break that touch barrier straight away with something that is socially acceptable. A quick, friendly hug will do. That's all you need to do when you first meet someone. It breaks the touch barrier straight away and then sets you up for the next stages...

So, when you are on your date, having a drink at a bar for example, this is when you want to escalate the touches even further. An easy example of this is when you are telling him a story, or something about your life, simply touch them whilst you are talking. A very brief touch...

For example, if you are sat down, you could say, 'You wouldn't believe what happened to me!', then at the same time, put your hand on his knee for a couple of seconds then take it off. Or you could touch his arm and do the same thing. It's under the radar and adds another time that you've broken the touch barrier, and it gets them more familiar with your touch.

Next, it's time to be a bit more calculated with it... Have these little canned lines ready in your mind; something that you have previously thought of to say that will break the touch barrier (a short routine if you will).

For example, saying to them, 'I love your rings, let me see.' Then extend your hand out (palm facing upwards). 9/10 times they will put their hand on top of yours because it's the normal thing to do. Then take their hand and look at their rings whilst holding their hand at the same time. Hand touching is a 1 level more intimate than a simple quick touch on the knee or arm.

Then throughout the date I want you to sprinkle in these little routines to keep building the level of comfort between you both. For example, you could say you like the smell of his aftershave, then ask him if you can smell it on him even closer. If he says yes, (which I'm sure he will), then lean in to smell his aftershave, but at the same time put your hand on his chest whilst you do it. He will find that attractive and it will get him hot under the collar.

Another one is that you could say that you love what he is wearing. Then at the same time you are complimenting him you can touch his clothes. This is very natural, and it breaks the touch barrier again. These things may seem small, but they will have a big impact!

The next step is when the first kiss happens. Because you would have been doing these socially acceptable touches throughout the date, the first kiss will feel very natural.

So, when they, or yourself, initiate the first kiss, be sure to use your hands as well. Embrace them with your hands. Don't just stand there with your hands hanging down by the side of your body. Instead, cup one hand on the side of his face whilst you kiss him. EVERY man loves this! You'll notice that because you have been continuously breaking the touch barrier, that the first kiss will feel effortless and not awkward at all.

If you are escalating the touch the correct way, it will feel very natural, and it will come under the radar. It will appear as if you are doing nothing at all. When in actual fact, you are doing a lot and building a lot more comfort and familiarity between you both. The art of building massive attraction should be to make everything feel as natural as possible between you both.

Cat String Theory

This is one of my favourite tips and it will get people much more attracted to you. The Cat String theory!

Ok, so I want you to visualise a cat in front of you, and yourself holding a piece of string...

If you throw that string on the floor and give the cat the string, then the cat doesn't care and loses interest.

If you take the string away and make it entirely out of reach of the cat, then the cat will lose interest in the string because the string is unattainable.

But if you dangle the string just in reach of the cat, teasing the cat so it thinks it can get the string if it makes an effort, the cat will go crazy for the piece of string.

Now apply this to the early stages of dating somebody new. If you fully give yourself to someone straight away, they will lose interest in you, and you will be appearing needy. If you appear as someone who is completely unattainable, then they won't pursue you because they believe that they have no chance with you. But, if you make it so you are attainable, but not giving yourself to them unless they work for it, you will be coming across as high value and they will want to pursue you.

For example, if someone says to you, 'Are you available tomorrow night for a date?', say back to them, 'I'm not, but I MIGHT be able the night after.' This makes it appear as though you aren't putting your life on hold for them. And when you say 'MIGHT' then that person will feel like it's more of a reward for them if they do manage to get you to go on a date with them that night.

Another good example is if you are on a 3rd, 4th, or 5th date with someone and you haven't had sex yet and you are having a heavy kissing session with them, you could say, 'IF you're lucky and play your cards right, you might get even more tonight.' This is a good use of 'Cat String Theory' because you are teasing them with the thought of sex, but they have to work for it a little bit because you've said, 'IF you're lucky and play your cards right'. It makes it so much more exciting for them because it will feel like a reward.

'Cat String Theory' can apply to texting too. Text them back too fast and too much and they will lose interest because you will appear needy. Take too long to text back or don't hardly text them at all, and they will lose interest because you will seem unattainable. But, if you get that nice balance where you text them enough to keep them interested and don't wait too long to reply, but don't reply instantly either, then they will feel like it's a healthy chase for them and they will pursue you.

'Cat String Theory' is brilliant for building attraction. And before you start thinking it... it's not playing games! It's a healthy way of maintaining the correct amount of interest that you give to someone, which gives them the opportunity to chase you and get rewarded for their efforts. Use it well and you'll have people craving you!

Challenge him to make yourself stand out

I want you to picture this...

There's a high value man who all women find attractive. He's goes on 10 dates with 10 different women. 9/10 women he goes on a date with are submissive to him and make it clear that he can have them any time that he wants them.

1/10 women will challenge him on what he says and mentally stimulate him. Also, this 1 woman doesn't throw herself at him and comes across as a challenge for him to get her romantically interested in him.

Now which woman do you think the man will be most attracted to?

That's right! The one woman who challenges him!

If a man gets A LOT of female attention, he becomes bored of it quite fast; and he will really crave a deeper connection with someone who is DIFFERENT to everyone else.

So, all you have to do is display to him that you are a challenge, and you won't always be submissive to him! If you can do this, I guarantee that he will find you so much more sexually attractive than all of the other women who throw themselves at him. He won't be able to stop thinking about you!

Another good thing about this is... High value men love a woman who can challenge them, however, low value weak men do NOT!

So, when you do challenge a man and aren't always submissive to him, then the lower value men will be scared off, whereas the higher value men will be more attracted to you. Thus, you've just saved yourself a lot of time because now you know who the high value men are that you should be dating!

Always be the person to end the first date

This tip is a simple one, yet so powerful at building attraction and putting yourself into a stronger frame.

All I want you to do on your first date with someone is... be the person who ends the date.

When you are on a date with someone and you have been there for a good amount of time, I want you to feel what the energy is like on the date... If the energy is feeling good and at a high point, I then want you to end the date. You could say something as simple as, 'I had a really nice time, but it's getting late, so I should go home.'

When you do this, you will be the person controlling the frame. And the frame of the interaction is that they are chasing you, and they will feel this. And because they feel like they are chasing you, they will be attracted to you.

You want to leave the date when the energy is at a good high point because people always remember how you last made them feel. And if the last feeling they had of you was a good one, then they will be very excited to see you again.

So being the person to end the date will make them feel like they are chasing you, which builds attraction, and it will make them feel even more excited to see you again.

It's so simple, yet works incredibly well when building attraction.

The Art of Being Smooth

Being smooth is a very special social skill to possess. Being smooth is an essential skill that you must learn if you want to be very successful when dating. It will really set you apart from everyone else.

In this chapter I am going to be giving you the tips and advice that you need in order to come across as a smooth, classy and charming character.

It will take a bit of practice, but once you become a smooth character everything will become 100 times easier for you when dating. People will become easily attracted to you, and flirting with other people will feel very natural to you.

Put all of these tips together and I promise you that you'll be one of the smoothest, classiest and most charming characters that people know...

Let them do the work

You need to let people know that you find them attractive, but at the same time appear that you can take it or leave it.

You need them to feel like they have to qualify themselves to you in order for you to take it further with them.

The main goal of this is to give them a subtle bit of interest to let them know that you are attracted to them, and then open the door for them to qualify themselves to you.

It's very easy to be smooth when you give someone the green light to flirt with you and then they start doing it. This is because you control the frame of the interaction, and it's hard to not be smooth from a dominant position like this.

This is done in a few ways… Here are a couple of examples for you…

1. Using your body language…

Give them a full body scan with your eyes so they see you doing it, then slowly turn away and smile… When you do this most people will understand that you are checking them out. By doing this you're letting them know that you find them attractive in a subtle way. It will give them the green light to flirt with you. Then once they actively start flirting with you, you then control the frame, and everything becomes much easier for you.

2. Using the 'Push-Pull technique'…

Say something as simple as, 'You're actually quite cute. Shame about the coat though…' Deliver this line in a fun, flirtatious manner. This works very well because you have given them interest, but then pulled away with a bit of teasing straight after. If they find you attractive, watch them qualify themselves to you and ask you questions about their coat and why you don't like it; or they might even try teasing you back. If they do this then you know that they find you attractive.

Once someone tries to impress you, or qualify themselves to you, all you have to do is let them do the work, and give them a little bit of interest back whilst gently teasing them at the same time. Do this and they will be putty in your hands.

They think they have good game, but in reality, it's your very subtle game of setting them up that is the good game.

When you're truly smooth it will appear as if you're doing nothing at all.

Be Unreactive

If you want to be a smooth character, being unreactive is super important. If you are somebody who reacts to everything and gets emotional very easily then you'll never come across as smooth.

A huge element of being smooth is appearing as if you have everything under control. If people can manipulate your emotions to get a reaction out of you, then it's impossible to be smooth.

It's simple... Don't be reactive to people. Take your time and do exactly what YOU want. Do things in your own time and don't let other people influence your actions and emotions.

Never make them feel pressured

One of the worst emotions you can invoke in someone when you are trying to be smooth around them is making them feel pressured.

Let's say you want to do something, but the other person doesn't, then you have 2 options…

The wrong option is to try and pressure that person into doing something. It makes them feel uncomfortable and awkward. Basically, it's the exact opposite of what someone who is smooth and charming would do. It makes the interaction feel as if you are going against the grain, and it makes you appear desperate and needy when you pressure people into doing things.

The correct way of getting people to do something that you want is by letting them do it because they WANT to do it. If someone doesn't want to do something, then never pressure them into it. Don't ask someone twice. Don't try and sell them on the idea of something. It makes you appear like you're trying too hard. Remember, the art of being smooth and charming is making everything appear effortless.

If someone doesn't want to do something just act like it's no big deal and no problem at all, and don't make them feel judged for it. Quickly change the topic of conversation to something that they enjoy.

Pressuring people to do things when they don't want to do it is just embarrassing. When you act the correct way, you'll make people feel a lot more comfortable around you and they will want to be in your company much more.

Escalate touch and dialogue the correct way

Being smooth is making everything seem effortless... You want to escalate things in a way with someone that before they know it, they have gotten to a place with you without even realising how they got there, and it feels natural and comfortable to them.

When you very first meet someone, you aren't going to run up to them and start making out with them. That would be very weird. But when you DO kiss them, you want it to feel very natural for them as if they have known you forever. So, if you haven't already, I want you to read the chapter, 'From the Dating Coaches Handbook' and the section 'Escalating the touch'. This will tell you exactly how to escalate the touch in a smooth manner in much more detail.

To escalate what you SAY in a smooth manner is very simple... Again, we aren't going to walk straight up to them and say, 'Wow, you're so hot!' That would be a bit weird... But instead, you want to subtly escalate the flirtations and conversation in a way where it feels normal to say to each other, 'You're so hot.' So, I want you to do this...

Start off the conversation with them in a normal manner. Then over time I want you to drop in small indicators that you find them attractive (body language, push-pull flirting techniques, small compliments etc). Build this up gradually...

Then over time when you feel like they are attracted to you, and the mood is right and they clearly find you very attractive because they are increasing the amount of compliments that they are giving you etc, then you can say things such as, 'You're so hot'...

HOWEVER, when you do deliver these more intense compliments, you need to deliver them in a manner that shows that it isn't a big deal for you to say these things. Don't deliver these compliments with a massive amount of emotion. Say it in a calm and flirtatious manner and I guarantee that even though it's an intense compliment, you'll come across as very smooth and confident, which is very attractive.

Take your time when escalating what you say to someone. Start off slow with small compliments and light flirting, then build it up to more intense compliments and flirting when you keep receiving indicators of interest back from them.

Rush it too much and you'll appear needy and overly keen. However, time what you say correctly, and you'll produce amazing results and appear smooth and very confident.

An easy way of putting it is like this...

Let's judge how intense a compliment is on the scale of 1-10.

1/10 being a compliment such as, 'You look nice'.

10/10 being a compliment such as, 'You are so HOT'.

If you start off by giving them a 10/10 compliment, then that's very direct and comes across as desperate. If you only ever give them 1/10 compliments, then that is boring. Instead, escalate your compliments like this...

(W= women, M= man)

W= 1/10
M= 2/10
W= 4/10
M=5/10
W=6/10
M=7/10
W=8/10
M=9/10
W=10/10
M=10/10

Always remember this... The secret to appearing smooth when giving a compliment and showing someone interest is to make it appear as if it's no big deal and you aren't nervous to give them that compliment or interest.

Also, never give them a compliment that shows significantly MORE interest than the interest that they are giving you. You want to give them a compliment that comes in just a little bit higher on the scale to escalate things. If they match you by escalating what they also say, then great and continue the game plan.

If they don't match your level of escalation, then you MUST wait for them to match your level of escalation. And if they don't also escalate what they are saying to you, then don't compliment them again until they do.

Basically you want to be rewarding their interest with your own interest, and meeting their disinterest with your own disinterest.

Most people get nervous escalating, but if you don't act nervous and escalate things they correct way, you'll come from a very strong frame and that's very smooth and sexy.

How to be smooth when flirting

A lot of people find it hard to flirt and be smooth at the same time... but once you know how, it's easy...

The secret to being smooth when flirting is to make it appear like they can get you, but at the same time they can't. This may sound confusing but it's not once you understand it...

If you make it appear like they can have you at any time that they want, then they will lose interest in you. Make yourself seem completely unattainable and they will also lose interest. But make it so it seems like they have a chance with you IF they impress you...

If you haven't already, please read the chapter 'From the Dating Coaches Handbook' and go to the sections titled 'Cat string theory' and 'The Push-Pull Technique'. This will teach you everything that you need to know about how to do this...

In a world where people are either too avoidant or too clingy, if you can make yourself have a nice balance of where someone can get you if they impress you, then you'll stand out from the crowd.

When flirting with someone, you want to give them a bit of interest, but always pull away and tease them after to get them chasing you...

The reason this makes you smooth is because you will be coming from a strong frame. All you then have to do is keep flirting and teasing them UNTIL they show A LOT interest to you; then you reward their flirtations by escalating your own flirtations.

You want someone to feel like it's an accomplishment when they get interest from you.

The secret to being smooth when flirting is giving them interest, but at the same time letting them know that they have to chase you a little bit if they want you. Remember, all men love the chase.

Slow everything down

This is the simplest tip for how to appear smooth and classy. Just slow everything down...

You want to slow down your body movements, so you appear relaxed. Even when you're feeling nervous, FAKE IT! When you fake it and move your body in a relaxed way, you will trick your mind into thinking that you are relaxed. Here are a few simple ways to appear more relaxed by using your body language...

- Sit back in your chair
- Don't be scared to take up space with your body
- Avoid jittery, nervous movements
- Move your body in a relaxed manner
- Never seem like you're in a rush

Do all of these things with your body and you'll appear

smooth and in control.

Now, your voice and tonalities... When talking, take your time. There's no need to rush. Nervous people talk very quickly. Relaxed people will take their time when talking, and they will use their pauses.

Also, don't come across as somebody who is too loud. It can be quite the turn off to many people. Talk in a relaxed, soft, controlled manner. Avoid those squeaky high pitches if you can!

If you can do all of these things you'll appear in control, relaxed, classy and very smooth.

Pick your words carefully

Your choice of words is incredibly important when it comes to whether someone thinks highly of you or not. There are a few factors that you must be aware of when speaking to appear smooth, classy and charming. I will break it down into 3 sections for you... Words that sound nice to the ear, your manners, and the art of being articulate...

Words to use that sound nice to the ear...

Each and every word has either a negative or positive connotation to it. You need to recognise whether the words that you are using has a negative or positive connotation when you are saying it.

For example, a word with a positive connotation would be, 'pleasant'. A word with a bad connotation would be, 'gross'. This may sound very obvious and rudimentary, but it's something that so many people tend to overlook.

When in conversation you only want to use words with positive connotations. Some words have more positive feelings associated to them than other words, yet they may have similar meanings.

For example, when you meet someone new you could say, 'It's NICE to meet you.' And that is ok, but it isn't as smooth and pleasant to the ear as saying, 'It's a PLEASURE to meet you.'

By using the word 'pleasure' instead of 'nice' you will be coming across as more charming. This is because if I said the word 'pleasure' to you, you brain would associate it with lots of positive things. For example, good sex, pleasurable food to eat, something very relaxing etc. Whereas, if I said the word 'nice' to you, then it wouldn't have as many strong positive connotations as the word 'pleasure'. It's an ok word to use, just not as good.

Another example is when you smell someone's perfume. You could say to them, 'You smell so good.' And that's a perfectly good compliment. But to make yourself sound more smooth and charming you could say, 'I adore your scent, I love it.'

The word 'smell' is an ok word to use, but 'smell' can have positive and negative connotations. Because when we don't like something, we would say 'That smells!'. But on the other hand, you could smell some very nice food and say, 'That food smells really good.' So, the word smell can be used in a good or bad way.

Whereas the word 'scent' is usually only associated with positive things in day-to-day language. When I think of the word 'scent' I think of flowers, or a good smelling perfume.

So, if I would ever be in a scenario where I have a choice of using the word 'smell' or 'scent' I would always pick 'scent'.

This may sound small, but I PROMISE you that if you get good at using words that only have positive connotations over words that can have negative connotations, you will come across so much more charming than everyone else.

Practice and experiment with different words and you'll get a feel for the correct words to use for different scenarios.

It really is a game changer, and it will make you appear so much classier.

Manners

The 2nd on the list of words to use when speaking relates to your manners...

In a world where having good manners is becoming rarer, having good manners is one of the most attractive traits that you can possess. There's nothing more unattractive to someone who DOES have good manners than somebody who DOESN'T.

We express our good manners in a few different ways, but what we SAY is one of them.

If you're on a date with someone and they forget their 'please and thankyous' it really is one of the biggest turn offs. It makes them seem unsocialised and it's embarrassing to be around them.

So this tip is simple, make sure that you express your manners through the use of words during a conversation and you'll come across much smoother, classier and way more charming.

Be articulate

And the 3rd tip is to be articulate...

Expand your vocabulary and be able to express exactly what you mean through your choice of words. Having a diverse vocabulary is one of the simplest, yet overlooked, components to making someone feel more attracted to you. Having a diverse vocabulary will make you come across as more intellectual and classier. To a VERY high value man these are both extremely important qualities that they will be looking for in a partner.

If you want an intellectual man (which I'm sure you do), then he will want to have a partner who is able to match him in conversation and intellect. So, all I want you to do is this...

Whenever you are describing something, try and use a more eloquent vocabulary to describe that thing. If you don't have a big vocabulary, then do a bit of research online to expand your vocabulary.

Let's say that you want to describe something as 'good to look at'... A more eloquent way of describing it would be by saying, 'It's captivating'.

This may sound small, and you may think it gets overlooked by people that you are talking to, BUT I PROMISE you that it doesn't.

When you start becoming articulate and using a larger vocabulary, people really start to take notice of you. They will see you as someone who is high value and intellectual. And if you want a high value intelligent man, you need to be able to display these traits.

A little secret of mine is that whenever I am speaking to new people, I will always express things using a more diverse and intellectual vocabulary than what I usually would use in my day-to-day life.

You only need to speak with a diverse intellectual vocabulary a few times when meeting new people because they will then see you as an intellectual, and they will treat you as such. Then once you start to become more familiar with that person, you won't need to express as many things with such a diverse vocabulary because they will already see you as an intellectual.

Doing all of these 3 tips together will really set you apart from everyone else and you'll come across as very smooth, classy and charming. Our choice of words is very powerful. You can either come across as someone who sounds very common, or actively make the choice to come across as someone who is very classy. I know which one I'd prefer to be viewed as! And before you know it, you'll be known as someone who is an interesting and eloquent speaker. And to a high value person, that is VERY attractive!

Always leave them wanting more

To be a truly smooth and charming character you need to learn the art of how to leave them wanting more. Know when to leave the conversation. Know when to pull away from the kiss. Know when to tease them physically. Know when to end the date so they crave the next date.

There's nothing more annoying than someone who overstays their welcome, or over does something to the point of it not being fun anymore. BUT a very smooth and charming trait to have is knowing when to leave things so it's leaves people wanting more.

The simple rule for how to leave them wanting more is this...

Always get people's emotions to a good high point, and then that is when you leave or stop what you are doing. Never overstay you're welcome in any scenario. A smooth character will feel when the energy is starting to dip, and they will know that's when it's time to leave or stop what they are doing.

People will always remember how you last made them feel. And if the last emotion they had of you is a positive one, they will want to be in your company again. Also, you'll never appear needy. Instead, it will appear as if they are chasing you. Plus, if you overstay your welcome in a conversation, or over do something, it will feel forced and a lot of effort. But if you leave when everything is good, they will feel no friction or boredom in your company, and it will appear as if everything you do is effortless. Because of this they will be excited for their next encounter with you…

Body Language

It's amazing what you can tell about somebody from their body language. People can hide what they are thinking and feeling with their words, but they can't hide it with their body language. Body language makes up about 80% of all human communication, so once you know what to look out for, it's like a having a social superpower. You'll know whether somebody finds you attractive, if they are excited by you, whether you should up your game, or even when it's the right time to go in for the kiss.
In this section I'll be giving you a few different examples of body language signals to look out for on a date and how to use it to your advantage...

If we scratch, we match

I love this one because not many people know about it, yet it's such a strong indicator of attraction. This was my first viral video on the internet because so many people realised that they do this or have seen it, but didn't know what it meant until now. Then once explained to them, they were saying, 'I DO THAT WHEN I THINK SOMEONE IS HOT!'

This piece of body language is more prominent in women, however many men still do this as well. So, it's well worth keeping an eye out for! So, here it is...

When you're talking to someone, stay aware of what their hands are doing. If they are looking at you and they GENTLY start scratching the back of their hands or collarbone, then this is a HUGE indicator that they feel attraction towards you (It must be a gentle scratch because hard scratching can indicate anxiety or stress).

The reason why we do this is because of evolution. Back when we were apes, we built social bonds by grooming each other. We would scratch ourselves as an invitation for someone to groom us to build stronger social bonds with them. This is something that is still hard wired into our DNA to this day.

So, if someone starts lightly scratching these places on their body in front of you, it's because they want to build strong social bonds with you because they find you attractive.

Obviously, we aren't going to start scratching each other, but it's our subconscious still asking the other person to groom us.

Now I've told you, you'll never be able to unsee it!

Pecking

Knowledge of Pecking can be used to your advantage massively when dating. It's a strong indicator that someone is into you.

So, what is Pecking? Pecking is when somebody leans in to talk to you, or to listen to you. The word pecking comes from birds. Putting their beak forward, to peck. Simple. So, this is what I want you to do when you're talking to someone...

I want you to NEVER peck when you are in a conversation with somebody, either when you are talking or listening to them. It can be perceived as low value behaviour. You're basically falling into their frame. BUT you can observe pecking to see if that person is into you or not...

When you are talking to someone, (it's usually more prominent when sitting down), I want you to lean back in your chair, then watch them... If they start pecking (leaning forward) to talk to you, that's a great sign that they are into you because it means they have fallen into your frame.

But you may be asking, 'What if I need to lean into them to hear them?'... Don't do it! Simply ask them to speak louder to you. Observe the pecking. Don't peck yourself.

You'll see so many people engage in pecking in social interactions, and you will now know who controls the frame between two people.

Mirroring

Mirroring is when somebody copies your body language. Usually, people will do this when they are in your frame, and it happens a lot when someone finds you attractive.

You can subtly test to see if someone finds you attractive by doing certain actions to see if they will copy you or not.

A very simple test is when you are having a drink with someone, take a sip of your drink and put it down. Repeat this a few times. If the other person does the same thing straight after you have, chances are they are mirroring you.

Another one you can do is cross your arms. If they do the same, they are mirroring you.

Another one is when you are sat at a table with them, lean your head into your hand, and if they do the same, they are mirroring you.

There are so many examples I can give of this. Experiment a little and have fun with it. Just know that if they copy your body language it's a great sign!

Slow everything down

This one is simple. SLOW EVERYTHING DOWN. Slow down the way you talk. Slow down your movements to make them smoother. Take your time.

People who are nervous or stressed tend to be twitchy in their movements, or they talk very fast because they just want to be finished with what they say. These are not attractive behaviours. Slow everything down and you'll appear much more confident and relaxed. Use your pauses when talking as well and they will think you've got everything under control. Just don't be TOO slow with everything though. Just make it seem natural.

Lip biting

We've all seen it in the movies. Someone finds someone else attractive, so they start biting their lip. Well, this is not just in the movies, it's actually true for real life too.

The reason why people will bite their lip when they find somebody attractive comes down to simple psychology. When we find somebody very attractive, we experience high emotions which create tension within our bodies. This tension needs to be released, and one of the ways this is released (when its tension from attraction), is to bite our lip. This is because the lips are a sensitive and intimate area of our bodies.

The other reason why people will sometimes bite their lip when they find someone attractive is because they want to kiss them. People will subconsciously bite their lip to draw your attention to their lips, so you start to think about kissing them, or other things...

Keep an eye out for this body language of attraction!

Arm behind the head to flex

This one is quite funny to observe. Men will do this one naturally without even noticing they are doing it. So, here it is...

When a man finds someone attractive, it's their natural instinct to want to appear strong and in good shape in front of their crush. Because of this they will put their hand behind their head and either scratch the back of their head or rest their hand there. They will then usually tense their arm.

This is to demonstrate that they have muscles to you. Sounds very primitive, but it's true. They will do this consciously; or sometimes they will even do this subconsciously, without them even realising they are doing it.

They do this in hopes that you will be impressed by their physique and find them attractive. Men will try to make this look natural, but we all know what they are trying to do...

What did that hug mean?

I'm going to give you two body language signs that people do in hugs that indicate attraction towards you. You can tell ALOT about how someone feels about you by the way they hug you. You can tell if they find you attractive, or if they don't feel any connection with you at all. But we are going to stick to the two body languages people do in hugs when they find you attractive...

The first one is the lingering hand... When someone hugs you and they find you attractive, they will want to touch you for as long as socially acceptable. Pay attention to what their hands are doing. When you pull away from a hug take notice if their hand slowly comes off your body, or if it slowly slips further down your body. This is done because they don't want to let go of you, and they want to keep touching you.

Another easy way to tell if someone finds you attractive when they hug you is this... When the hug is about to come to an end, they will give you a little bit of a tighter squeeze. This is because they want to get as close to your body as socially acceptable. It's fast and can be subtle, but it means a lot.

Also, a quick little tip about hugging in the early stages is... if, most of the time, you are the one to pull away from the hugs before they do, then the other person will fall into your frame, and they will feel (on a subconscious level) that they are chasing you. This makes you seem more attractive to that person...

Exposing their neck to you

This piece of body language comes straight out of the animal kingdom. When all is said and done, we are animals, and this piece of body language is still in our DNA...

When you're talking to someone, pay attention to what they are doing with their neck. If at some point during the conversation, they tilt their head a little and expose their neck to you, it's a great sign!

This is often done subconsciously and means that they are feeling submissive and/or comfortable around you. You have basically made that person feel very relaxed in your company.

The reason why we do this is because our necks are a very vulnerable part of our body. We expose it for submissive reasons to show the other person that we are no threat, and we want them to know we are submissive towards them in that moment.

Or, the other reason is, that we want to display to that person that we are very relaxed around them and it's a subconscious body language we do because we want them to know that.

Don't underestimate understanding this piece of body language, because it will often tell you if that person is relaxed around you.

Touching the hair

So, a lot of people already know that if someone finds another person attractive, they will start touching their hair, or fiddling with their hair. This is more prominent in women; however, a large majority of men do this behaviour as well.

You may be asking yourself, 'Why do we touch our hair when we find somebody attractive though?'

It comes down to evolution. Our hair is a health indicator of how good our health is, how much nutrients we are getting, good genetics etc. And the reason why we touch our hair when we find someone attractive is to bring the attention of that person to our hair, and ultimately show off just how healthy we are. This is because we are designed by evolution to seek out partners who are healthy so that we have a better chance of having stronger babies who will survive.

Obviously, with modern science we know that health varies in every person, and that hair does not tell us everything about someone's health. But this behaviour to judge someone's 'healthiness' by their hair is still hard wired into our brains from thousands of years of evolution.

So, if you see someone start brushing their hands

through their hair (which is what most men do), or fiddling with their hair when talking to you, then chances are their body language and subconscious is saying to you, 'Hey, look at how healthy I am. Find me attractive because I find you attractive'.

The eyes don't lie

It's true, the eyes don't lie. You can tell a lot about what someone is thinking by the way they move their eyes. Do they find you attractive? Are they lying to you? Are they happy? And much more. But here are 3 simple eye movements that are a strong indicator that someone finds you attractive...

1. The Eye Pop - When someone finds you attractive, and they look at you, it will look like their eyes pop and widen, and they get taken back a bit. This is their brains way of getting a better look at someone they find attractive, and it's usually done involuntarily.

2. The Full Body Scan - When someone finds you attractive, they will look up and down your body very quickly. They may do this even when you are mid conversation with them. It's very hard to resist giving someone a full body scan when you find them attractive. Keep a look out for this because this one happens ALL the time!

3. The Eye Pop, then a sudden look at the floor, then looking side to side when looking at the floor - Ok, so we know why they do the eye pop, but sometimes it's followed up by the eyes looking downwards, then side to side at the floor... The reason why they look side to side when looking at the floor is because people do this

when they are having an inner dialogue with themselves. Basically, talking to themselves in their head! And if it's happening after the eye pop, then I pretty much guarantee they are thinking about how attractive they think you are!

Surrogate touching

This is an interesting body language to observe.

I'm sure you've seen scenes in a movie or on TV where someone is flirting, and they start playing with their straw seductively in their drink, or slowly fiddling with an item. Well, that's called surrogate touching. People will start playing and fiddling with things in a slow and seductive manner when they find someone attractive. Keep an eye out for it next time you're talking to someone.

The reason why people do this is because it is a release of sexual tension that they feel inside themselves. So, they will project their feelings unconsciously onto an object when they are talking to you.

Also, you can tell when someone is nervous. For example, they will start fiddling with things in a fast manner and get a little jittery. But when someone finds you attractive, it is a done in a slow and seductive manner. Fascinating to watch!

Different Ways to break the Touch Barrier

Breaking the touch barrier is a significant step when meeting someone new. Sometimes it can happen naturally, sometimes it can be awkward, and sometimes it can feel strange, but my goal is to teach you how to do it in a smooth and easy way.

The great thing about breaking the touch barrier earlier on during a date is that it will make you both feel so much more relaxed and familiar around each other. Also, when you go to escalate into more touching with each other, such as when you kiss them, it will feel so much more natural and enjoyable for the both of you. Plus, it's a great way to flirt with someone. Let's get into different ways to break the touch barrier...

Compliment what they are wearing

Let's say you're on a date with someone and you love their shirt... You could either say to them, 'I love what you're wearing', or you could see it as an easy opportunity to break that touch barrier...

Simply say to them, 'I love what you're wearing', then at the same time gently grab a piece of their clothing on their arm, and then gently let it go. Don't hold onto it for too long though, it should only last a couple of seconds.

They will notice this, and it will add to the effects of the compliment whilst getting them hot under the collar at the same time. It will come across as flirtatious and if they think you're hot, it will work wonders for you.

A quick touch on the knee

This must be done whilst sitting down with someone, for obvious reasons!

When you're sat down talking to someone, I want you to do this... Start a conversation, and at the same time put your hand on their knee whilst you are talking to them.

For example, you could say to them, 'You wouldn't believe what happened to me!', then put your hand on their knee at the same time, whilst holding eye contact with them. Hold it for about 3 seconds then take it off. Then carry the conversation on as normal.

It's subtle, but trust me, they will be thinking about that touch and how nice it felt to have your hand on their knee/leg, even if it was only for a couple of seconds.

Because it's done fast, it's socially acceptable and comes across very normal. However, it has a very powerful effect!

‘Oh, I love your jewellery’

I love this one. It works so well at breaking the touch barrier in a very subtle way.

Let’s say you’re on a date and the person you’re on a date with is wearing a nice watch, or a nice bracelet, or rings etc. This is a perfect chance to break the touch barrier and compliment them at the same time.

Simply say to them, ‘Oh I love your jewellery, let me see’. Then extend your hand with your palm facing upwards, inviting them to place their hand on top of yours.

When you do this most people will put their hand on top of yours because it’s normal to do so. Then you can look at their jewellery and move their hand around yours to get a closer look.

This is a great way of breaking the touch barrier in a normal way, and it makes them feel good about their fashion choices at the same time. It’s a win-win!

Hug to say hello

This may sound very basic, but when you meet them, give them a quick and friendly hug hello. It’s socially normal and they will hug you back.

The reason why we do this is because it breaks the touch barrier straight away, and allowing for other times when you touch them on the date to feel much more comfortable.

It may sound simple, but that doesn’t mean it doesn’t

work! Make sure to hug them when you say hello!

Nice Hands

All men love this one and it's super easy to do...

Say to him, 'Your hands look so big, show me.' Then put your hand out.

Naturally he will put his hands on top of yours to show you how big his hands are, then say to him, 'I absolutely love that you have big hands.'

He will love this because it will make him feel masculine and it's an easy way to break the touch barrier. Works every time!

The Secret to the Perfect First Kiss

The first time you kiss someone can be a big deal! But there are some very simple rules that you need to follow to ensure that the first kiss is done smoothly, and leaving them wanting to kiss you again and again...

When do I kiss them?

Timing is very important when going in for the first kiss. Too soon and you'll come across as too keen. Too late and the other person will be questioning whether you think they are attractive. So, when should you go in for the first kiss?

Rule 1: Go in for the kiss when the energy is good between you both. Never go in for the kiss when the energy is at a low point. You want the kiss to be associated with positive emotions. So, let's say you are having a highly flirtatious conversation, looking at a beautiful view, or they are giving you all the right body language signals; then that's when you go in for the kiss!

Rule 2: 'When during the date do I go in for the kiss?'... Going in for a kiss at the end of the date isn't a bad thing, but it does put pressure on it and makes the first kiss feel a little bit planned, awkward and uninspired.

So, it's simple... Have a rough idea of when the date will end, let's say 10pm. The best time to go in for the first kiss is around 75% of the way through the date. That's right, not the end, but 75% of the way through. The reason is because the first kiss will then feel spontaneous and more exciting.

The second thing it does is that it sets the tone for the remaining 25% of the date. You'll feel much more relaxed around that person and will have overcome an important step in getting to know each other physically.

And thirdly because you've already had a kiss earlier on during the date, when you kiss them again when saying goodbye, you'll be more relaxed and familiar with each other, so the last kiss will be much better. Trust me on this... Watch how they change to be much more relaxed around you after you have had the first kiss.

Rule 3: 'Do I kiss them on the first date?'... If you like them and you WANT to kiss them, then absolutely, 100% YES! Remember, kissing is comfort building, not seduction (heavy make out sessions are seduction).

If you don't kiss them for too many dates, the other person may think you only see them as a friend. Also, if you wait too long to kiss them, it puts massive pressure on the first kiss, and I guarantee you won't enjoy it as much.

How do I initiate the First Kiss?

There are many ways to go in for the first kiss in smooth manner that they'll love. I know a lot of women like the man to make the first move for the first kiss, but if you are getting all the right signals, and you are the one to initiate the first kiss, then that raw confidence can make you stand out! And to the right guy that is extremely sexy.

Here are some rules to follow on how to initiate the first kiss...

Rule 1: Make sure you've broken the touch barrier earlier on during the date. THIS IS VERY IMPORTANT if you want that first kiss to feel like you've known each other for a long time, and it will make the first kiss feel very natural. This can be done in many ways. Revisit the tips and advice on how to break the touch barrier during the date if you're forgetting, as it will make your first kiss so much better!

Rule 2: Don't make it awkward! Here are some simple tips on how to initiate the first kiss in a smooth manner...

Read their body language

Start off my reading their body language. If they keep looking at your eyes, then lips, then eyes again, and they keep repeating this body language when you are talking to them, they are doing this because they are thinking about kissing you. This is a good indicator of interest.

When the vibe and energy is good, say to them, ‘So, do you ever kiss on the first date?’ Make sure to deliver this in a fun, light, flirtatious manner for it to be effective. If the energy is good, chances are they will say ‘yes’. That’s when you go in for the kiss.

Make a fun moment out of it

Another way to initiate the first kiss is to make a fun moment out of it. Let’s say you are playing a game with them. Any game. Say to them that you want to make a fun little bet. It makes the game more fun.

Of course, they will say, ‘What do you want to bet for?’

And then all you have to say is, ‘Well, I’ll decide that if I win.’

If they say, ‘You have to tell me’, just say back to them,

‘Well that’s a secret, but don’t worry, it won’t be something too mean.’

Deliver this in a fun way. Then if you win, say to them,

‘Ok, I won. So, my bet was that if I win, you have to kiss me.’

Then if they think you are attractive, they’ll go in for the kiss. If you lose, they will say,

‘What was your bet?’

Then admit it was a plan to kiss them. If they like you, they will kiss you anyway. It's a win-win situation for you to be in!

Ask them!

This one is simple... Ask them if they want a kiss!

If you notice that they are giving off all the right signals, then simply saying to them, 'Can I kiss you?', can be very endearing and cute.

Make sure that when you ask them, that the energy is at a high point to ensure the result that you want.

If they say, 'No', don't worry, just brush it off and act cool about it and say, 'I only asked because I couldn't tell if you were giving me that energy or not'.

But by saying this, it puts the thought of kissing you in their mind.

Be confident when you ask them, and you will get a better response than you may think!

The Kissing Tip that went viral on the internet!

I love this tip. It's one of my favourite pieces of dating advice that went viral across the internet with people saying how incredibly well it worked for them. So, here it is...

When you are sharing the first kiss with someone, do this... Always make sure that you are the FIRST person to pull away from the kiss...

When you do this, you control the frame of the interaction, and the frame of the interaction is that they are chasing YOU! And because they feel like they are chasing you, they will want to kiss you again and again.

Try this out and see for yourself. It works amazingly

well!

Use your hands too!

Do something with your hands! Don't have your hands by your sides. Instead do something with them! Cup their face with one hand whilst you bring them in closer with the other. This always makes the kiss feel much more intimate and sexier...

Red Flags

Red flags are everywhere in the dating world! The red flags that you ignore today are the reasons why you end things with someone tomorrow. Some red flags are very obvious to notice. Whereas some red flags take a bit more of trained eye to see.

The thing about red flags is that when people leave relationships that didn't work out, they always look back and say how obvious the red flags were that they didn't notice when they were in the relationship. It's because people are full of emotions when in a new relationship that they don't see things for what they really are.

In this section I am going to be talking about the different red flags that there are out there that you should never ignore if you want to be in a loving happy relationship. I hope this helps you in your dating life or an existing relationship that you are in...

The Love Bomber

This is one of the most known red flags in dating, but it's

surprising at how many people still ignore it...

A love bomber is somebody who showers you in words of affirmation, affection, promises and overall someone who is very full on in the early stages of dating.

This is a red flag because love bombers will always be like this at the start, and then once they've got you hooked, they will treat you badly. This creates a dynamic where your emotions are always up and down, and then you become reliant upon them for the positive emotions that you once felt in the early stages from them. Then when they ignore you and they are dismissive towards you, it makes you feel like you've done something wrong, so you try to please them to get the positive emotions from them again.

People who are too giving and proclaim their love for you too early on always have a secret agenda. Unfortunately, it works on a lot of people, because people think that they have found someone who thinks the world of them. When in reality, they are setting them up to be hooked on the idea of this 'Prince Charming', but once they got them hooked, they will treat them badly and make them reliant upon themselves for the positive emotions they once felt in the relationship, thus creating a dynamic where they have a lot of control. People do this because they are manipulators. This is because of their narcissistic personality.

Think about it... Why would you give someone everything, proclaim your love for someone, and shower them in a lot of affection and words of affirmation so soon after getting to know them? You wouldn't because you don't even really know that person yet! The only reason people do this is because they have a hidden agenda.

If you think someone is being too full on and telling you everything that you want to hear too soon after only knowing you for only a short amount of time, be aware! You may have someone trying to love bomb you!

When he tells you what you can or can't wear

Urgh... I hate this one so much. This is such a controlling behaviour that some men have towards women. For example, a woman is going on a night out and she likes wearing clothes that show a little bit of skin, then the man she is dating starts getting angry and upset about it.

This has absolutely NOTHING to do with the woman. This all comes from his own insecurities. He doesn't have much confidence in himself and is a jealous character. He believes that if a woman dresses sexy, that other men will approach her and flirt with her.

Yes, this may be the case and men might try to flirt with her... But if he treats her nicely and sees himself as a high value man, he will know that he has nothing to fear because his partner loves and respects him. Because of this, she would never cheat on him and reject all the other men that try to flirt with her.

But the thing is... if a woman complies to her partners demands and dresses how HE chooses, then it will only get worse with time. This controlling behaviour will lead to more severe controlling behaviours because he had a tantrum and got his own way, so he will start doing this in other areas of the relationship; and before you know it, you'll be in a miserable and abusive relationship.

If a man starts getting mad at you for dressing in a certain way, you MUST say this to him... 'I will dress how I want, don't push your insecurities onto me, I will not be controlled by you. Do not tell me what I can or can't wear because if you do it again, I'm leaving this relationship.' And if he starts an argument after that, then walk away. However, if he apologises and never does it again, then great. If he doesn't apologise and doesn't correct his behaviours, then walk away from the relationship.

As a dating coach, I have seen many bad relationships where people try controlling their partner's life choices. Don't let that be you!

A confident man will not care how you dress because he knows that he is a high value man and that you won't cheat on him. Trust me on this... A confident man will love it if you dress sexy. He will show you off to the world!

When he tells you who you can or can't be friends with

This is a very dangerous red flag that you must never ignore. This is an abusive person's way of isolating you and controlling you. If they can, they will get you away from all of your friends and make you dependent upon themself, so that you become very easy for that person to control.

They will always target your most outspoken friends first and tell you that they are bad for you etc, and that you shouldn't talk to them. This is because they are the friends who will speak out most against them. Then over time they will start to do this with everyone.

They will also want you to stop spending as much time with friends and will guilt trip you into spending more time with them instead. This is because it naturally separates you from your friends.

A good partner will love it that you have friendships and will encourage you to see your friends.

NEVER ignore this red flag!

The guy who talks about his 'trauma' after only knowing you for a short amount of time

This is a red flag that so many people ignore at the start because they think that people are just opening up about their lives. Do not fall for it. People who have actual trauma never want to talk about their trauma until they are comfortable and feeling safe around someone. But most people with bad trauma won't want to talk about it at all.

So, you may be asking yourself, 'Why do people tell me about their traumas so soon?' The reason is actually quite a sinister one. It's to make you feel pity for them, so you become easier to manipulate. They will try using their stories of their 'trauma' to trigger your feelings of pity. So, when they act in a bad way, they will use their 'trauma' as an excuse to fall back on. And if you don't accept their behaviour because of these 'traumas' they have been through, they will make you out to be a bad person.

So, if someone you've just started dating starts telling you stories of all these bad traumas they have been through, it is most likely a lie and you need to ask yourself, 'Why are they really telling me this?'

Well now you have the answer... It stems from when they are younger and these behaviours worked on other people, so they do these behaviours their whole lives because they find people are easier to manipulate when they feel sorry for them.

The time waster and excuse maker

We have ALL met someone like this. They waste our time and have an excuse for EVERYTHING! This can be terribly frustrating.

If someone arranges a date with you and they cancel, but they have a good excuse and they are genuinely apologetic, then let them off. Once is ok if the excuse is good enough. BUT when in the early stages of dating them, only let them off ONCE. Unexpected things in life happen and that's ok. But, if they cancel two times in a row when dating you, do not waste your time talking to that person again. Once is a mistake, twice is on purpose.

On a sidenote... If someone stands you up on a date, or cancels at the very last minute, then delete and block their number. They are not worth your time at all!

Some people like to do this to others because they like the validation that they receive when they feel wanted, even though they never had the intention of going on the date. These types of people always come up with the most absurd excuses too. Do yourself a favour and move on from this person. They aren't worth your time or effort.

Late for a date

This guy really doesn't care about your time...

I say, 5 minutes late can be let off if he apologises and he has a good excuse. If he's 10 minutes late, then he better have a good excuse and be very apologetic. 15 minutes late, without a GREAT excuse, then leave the date.

A gentleman will always arrive to a date 5-10 minutes early because a gentleman will never want to leave a lady waiting. It's basic manners.

If he is late because traffic was genuinely awful because there's been a road accident for example, then let him off. But if he was late because of his poor time management... then trust me, he's not the one. He clearly doesn't see your time as valuable as his own. Also, it's just so rude!

He talks too much about his ex who he apparently 'hates'

Have you ever been on a date with a man who talks too much about his ex? Well, a lot of people have. This is a big red flag. If he is talking about his ex a lot on a first date, then he's definitely not over her.

If he starts calling his ex names such as 'psycho' on a first date, this is also a big red flag. It shows a lack of social awareness (because clearly you don't want to talk about his ex), it shows he clearly isn't over her, it shows he is self-centred because he's talking about himself instead of getting to know you, and it's just plain weird.

If a guy does this on a date with you, the best thing you can do is to not see him again.

He doesn't respect your boundaries

Everybody should have clear boundaries when dating. Things that you think are acceptable and things that you don't. When dating, it is very important that you are clear about your boundaries with people when they are crossing them, because people have very different opinions on what is and what isn't acceptable.

It's important that you pay attention to how someone reacts when you say 'NO' to them. Do they get annoyed, hostile, or aggressive? Or do they respect your boundaries and listen to you and act accordingly? Someone who will ignore your boundaries is someone who you don't want to be dating.

He talks about his previous sex life to you in detail

This one is a red flag for two reasons...

Reason 1 - When you have sex with someone, I believe that what goes on between you both, stays between you both. Basically, an unwritten rule of privacy between you both. Like the old saying goes, 'A gentleman doesn't kiss and tell'. If he starts telling you in detail about his sex life with previous partners... Well... If you have sex with him, he most certainly will tell everyone all about the sex that you two have together. Do you really want everyone knowing what you get up to in the bedroom?

Reason 2 - It shows that he isn't socially aware. If you're on a date with him and he starts talking in detail about his previous sex life, it shows that he isn't properly socialised.

Is that really the type of man you want to be dating?

Mr. Self-centred

We all know someone like this... They only talk about themselves and don't really care what you have to say or what goes on in your life.

When talking to a guy, really pay attention to how he listens and responds to you. Is he actually listening so he can understand what you are saying and add value to the conversation? Or is he waiting for you to stop talking so he can carry on talking about himself? Does he ask you about your day? Does he ask you questions about your life? Does he genuinely seem to want to get to know you, or is he more interested in telling you about himself?

Your date (or partner) should be asking you questions to get to know you; not be obsessed with themselves.

Do yourself a favour and date someone who cares about you and others, not just themselves. You'll be much happier with a partner like that.

He hides you from his friends and family

This red flag comes up a lot with people who are cheaters. A man who hides you from his friends and family is ALWAYS up to no good.

The main reason why they hide you away is because they have other girlfriends, or they are talking to other women, and he doesn't want the women finding out about each other.

He will always come up with excuses like, 'I'm a private person and I don't want anyone knowing my business' or 'I'm just not at that stage in the relationship yet'.

If it has been a couple of weeks and he doesn't want to let people know that he's been dating you, then ok, let him off, as some people do value privacy. But if you two have been dating for a while and he still won't tell anyone about you, then he is definitely up to no good.

Trust me on this, if someone is being secretive about who they are dating, it's always a bad sign.

He still talks to his ex

BIG RED FLAG! If your partner is still talking to their ex, this is not a good thing.

There are only 2 reasons when it is acceptable for them to talk to their ex.

The first reason is when they have children with their

ex, so they must communicate. If they get on with their children's other parent, that's great if no boundaries are crossed, then everyone is a winner.

The only other time it's acceptable is if they work with their ex. Same again, if they are platonic with each other and no boundaries are crossed, then that is also ok.

That's the only two times I would say where it is ok for your partner to be in contact with their ex.

If they talk to their ex outside of these two situations, then it's disrespectful to your relationship. There needs to be boundaries in a relationship, and this is one of them. Why would you want your partner to be talking to someone they have been intimate with before? Most people would say they wouldn't.

If someone stays in contact with their ex outside of the two reasons that I have given, it's because they aren't over each other yet. There is still something that is pulling them both towards each other, and I guarantee it's more than just being friends.

You don't want to find yourself in a love triangle with your partner and his ex. That's a terrible place to be. Don't date someone who still talks to their ex, apart from the 2 reasons I have said that are acceptable! It never ends well!

Is he buying my love?

Getting gifts can be a nice thing. But there is a limit to what should be given. If you haven't known someone for a long time and they are getting you a lot of gifts or buying you expensive things, this is a red flag.

Many people fall into the trap of thinking, 'They are getting me gifts, so they must like me, because this is how they express it.' Little thoughtful gifts are nice here and there, but lavish expensive gifts, or ALOT of gifts, then it's a bad sign.

The reason why people will give you a lot of gifts or spend a lot of money on you, is because it's a way for them to control you. They are trying to get you to feel indebted to them. They are trying to make you feel like you owe them something. This is a manipulation technique of theirs. Then when you do something that they don't agree with, they will always throw it back in your face that they bought you all of these nice things hoping that it makes you feel guilty, so you end up behaving exactly how they want you to instead.

Trust me, this happens ALL of the time with these types of people.

Also think about it... Why would someone who has a good personality and who is high value need to buy you a lot of expensive things?

It shows that they know their personality isn't enough to keep you interested in them.

This is always a red flag that people tend to overlook. As the saying goes, 'There's no such thing as a free lunch'.

Watch how he treats the other women in his life (This can also be a green flag)

You can tell a lot about how a man is going to treat you by

the way he treats other women who are close to him in his life, such as his mother and sisters.

A lot of how a man acts towards women when he is older comes from what he learns when he is young. When he was young, if he was never disciplined when he disrespected women, he will continue to disrespect women when he is older because he will think it is acceptable behaviour.

But, if he had good parents who taught him right and wrong, he will be a lot more likely to treat the women that he grew up with, with the respect that they deserve, and will continue this behaviour when he is an adult.

So, if he is nice to the women who are close to him, 99% of the time, chances are that he's going to be nice to you. If he isn't nice to them, chances are that he will repeat that behaviour in his future relationships too.

The man with a high 'body count'

When I say a high body count, it's referring to the amount of people he has had sex with.

If a man has a high body count, RUN! You are wasting your time if you are looking for a long-term relationship with him. A high number body count will tell you a lot about how he views relationships. If a man has a high body count it will show you these a few things...

1. He has sex with women that he doesn't think are good enough to settle down with. (Just because HE doesn't see them as a high value partner, it doesn't mean they aren't. He more than likely has an inflated ego and sees himself as far better than he really is. This usually stems from a

superiority complex).

If a man has been with a lot of women, why doesn't he want to settle down with any of them? Perhaps he isn't picking women who he sees as good enough to be his girlfriend? And if that is the case, he must not value his own time to be spending it with someone who he doesn't value enough.

So, in actual fact, if this is the case, he is a very low value man himself, and it actually has no reflection on the women's value that he is having sex with. A high value man is very selective about who he spends his time with.

2. He has commitment issues. He doesn't want to settle down because he is scared of being committed. Don't waste your time on him if this is the case.

3. He's a narcissist. He only cares about himself and having quick sexual encounters, and he doesn't care if the other person gets emotionally attached to him. If that is the case, he will be the type of man to tell a woman everything that she wants to hear in order to have sex with her, then he will usually ghost her.

4. No woman wants to settle down with him. He may be a good looking guy, or be great when you first meet him, but then the real him comes out, and then the women who he sleeps with lose attraction for him, and then leave him.

5. He views women as something that is purely sexual for him to play with. If you feel this is the case, just run from him. He's not worth your time as these types don't change, and they are very bad people.

6. He may not be that intelligent. A study was done where the results were concluded that intelligent people seek

things that are good for them in the long term, whereas people with less intelligence acted upon impulse because they favoured short term satisfaction over a long term one. So, he might just be dumb.

7. He's far more likely to cheat in a relationship. A man who has a high body count will be so much more likely to cheat when things get a little bumpy in the relationship. Instead of working through things with their partner, they are more likely to seek sex and comfort with someone else because it's what they are used to.

So, if you think getting with a man with a high body count is a good thing, think again! Let's say he's had sex with 100 women... You really think that he's going to start changing his ways at number 101? No chance. Get someone who values long term relationships, and you'll have much more success when dating.

Mr. Jealous and possessive

We have all met a man who is jealous and possessive at some point. There are different types of jealousy, but I will keep it just to these two that are red flags. So, most jealousy comes from one's own insecurities. Let's start off with the first type of jealousy...

I want you to pay close attention to how a man reacts whenever you tell him good news. This will tell you a lot about him.

When you tell him good news and he reacts genuinely happy for you, celebrates with you, wants to find out more and makes you feel good about your good news, then GREAT!

But, when you tell him good news and his energy seems a little off, he isn't happy for you, starts bragging or talking about himself, tries to one up you on your good news, doesn't seem to want to celebrate your good news and just overall acting like he really isn't interested, it's because he is jealous and self-centred.

This is because he is insecure, and he feels like you are beating him, and it makes him feel bad about himself. So, he becomes jealous inside. Sometimes he will hide this, but the cracks will always start to show.

Your partner should be super happy when you tell him good news. You are a team. If he doesn't see your good news as something to celebrate, you're in a relationship with the wrong person.

The other type of jealousy I am going to talk about is the type where they get jealous of other men, or you spending time with your friends.

This 100% stems from their own insecurities. If he gets jealous when another man tries to talk to you (and you have absolutely no control if that man has tried talking to you), or if he gets angry when you go on a night out because other men will look at you, it's because he is insecure because he has no confidence in himself.

Also, if he gets jealous when you spend time with your friends and not him, that is also jealousy because he wants your time, and it's also him displaying a possessive personality. So, he projects those feelings into the relationship and it makes for an extremely toxic relationship.

Let's talk about when he is possessive... It's such a terrible trait for him to have. When someone is possessive it can be abusive and a gate way into even more abusive behaviours. If he is trying to control where you go, who you spend your time with, what you're doing etc, then you must get out of that relationship ASAP! This behaviour can come from jealousy, insecurities, a poor upbringing, and many other reasons.

Either way, if he is being possessive towards you, then leave that relationship before it turns into something even more sinister. You're nobody's possession, and if they think like that, they are not the one for you.

He is looking for a mother, not a lover

This is such a common red flag these days that often gets overlooked. So many men out there are looking for a mother, not a lover. A big indicator of this is when you go and visit his home. If his house is dirty and untidy, then it's a huge red flag...

You got to think about it like this... If he knew that you are going over to his, then surely, he would have cleaned up before. And 9/10 times, this is the cleanest he is going to be. If his house is still dirty and untidy, then he is 100% looking for a mother, not a lover. He wants someone to tidy up after him and do the housework.

Also, if he doesn't know how to do laundry, cook for himself, tidy the house, and asks you to do it when you are dating him, then don't waste your time with him, otherwise you'll take over the role of his mother.

It's not a sexy or healthy type of relationship for you

to be in. He's a full-grown man. He should be able to do all these things himself and actually take pride in himself and his home.

Mr. Overly Sexual

There is a very easy way to tell if a man wants you just for sex, or if he's actually serious about looking for a relationship...

First of all, if before you have even been on a date with him, and he makes any sexual remarks towards you, then I 100% guarantee that he just wants you for sex. If he is looking for a relationship and an actual connection with someone, then he will get to know them before talking about sex. Plus, it shows he's a little socially inept if he thinks talking about having sex with you, or any innuendos like this, is appropriate socialising at this early stage.

Another indicator is if he invites you to his house, or asks to go to your house on a first or second date. There is only one thing on his mind... Having sex with you.

If he asks you to go to his home on the first date, it's very clear that he only wants you for sex. But, if he asks you to his home on the second date, it's because he is being more calculated about it. He uses the first date as a formality to trick you into thinking that he isn't after you for sex. When in reality, he has planned to get your hopes up and make you think that he is looking for a relationship to make you more willing to sleep with him on the second date.

9/10 times after they have had sex with you, their

mannerisms towards you change and it leads to them ghosting you or telling you that they don't feel a spark etc. So, if a guy ever invites you back to his on a first or second date or makes sexual comments early on, then that's a red flag that you must not ignore if you're looking for a relationship.

Green Flags

We have all heard of Red flags. But what about Green Flags? Green Flags are indicators that someone is a good person. There are many different green flags to look out for when dating.

In the world of modern dating, it can be easy to just be on the lookout for red flags because, let's be honest, there's a lot of people out there who have them. But there are some amazing people who have no red flags and only have green flags who would be perfect for you!

So, in this section I'm going to teach you the Green flags that people have, so you can recognise when somebody will make the perfect partner for you...

No mixed signals

It may sound simple, but if they like you, you will know, and they will show it.

Men who display mixed signals are either playing games or just really not that into you. Whereas if a man doesn't show any mixed signals, it's a great sign. It shows that he has the right mindset. He doesn't like leaving people in limbo and wondering whether he likes them or not.

He makes an effort to make you feel wanted and desired when dating. He doesn't leave you guessing whether he is getting with other women. He shows you what he wants, and that is you!

He makes an effort with you

A huge green flag is when someone makes effort with you. They plan dates, they make the effort to communicate with you, they plan out their schedule so they can spend time with you, and many other examples just like these.

It's simple, if he makes the effort, it's a huge green flag!

He has a history of long-term relationships

You can 99% of the time predict what people will be like in their relationships by looking at their past.

If he has a history of long-term relationships and doesn't sleep about with lots of different people, it's a green flag. This shows that he values long-term relationships and chooses to look for this when dating, instead of quick flings with people. It also shows that he has a mindset that is more orientated to seek out long term goals in his own life.

Another bonus to dating a man who has a history of long-term relationships is that he will usually be more mature when handling the relationship during tough times.

It also shows that women want to keep him around for a long time, and it shows that he can keep a woman, instead of the women he's dated in the past getting rid of him because he is up to no good etc.

So, when you're finding out about a guy and he says that he has a history of long-term relationships, be happy, because that's a green flag right there!

Good with money

Now, I'm not saying you should ever value a man by his finances because I don't think you should, because things happen in life and money comes and goes. So, it's not about how much he has. It's about how he handles his money that matters.

You can tell a lot about a person by the way they handle their money. For example, if he owes his friend some money and doesn't pay him back, but instead goes out and spends his money on stupid things instead of paying his friend back, that's a huge red flag. It shows that he is selfish and inconsiderate. But, if he's someone who would pay his friend back the instant he has the money, then that's a green flag.

Another example is if he is putting financial strain on you by asking you to pay for things unfairly when he has the money himself... That's a HUGE red flag.

Another red flag is when he is asking you to pay for things that he doesn't need.

Also, another red flag is when instead of going out and earning his own money (or at least trying), he asks you to buy him things.

But it's a green flag if he doesn't put financial strain on you in any way.

This becomes important when you start living together. You don't want to be with a man who splurges all his money away, so you're left there wondering if you can afford the heating or electric bill. That would be a nightmare!

Instead, you want him to be aware of his outgoings and income. Does he pay for more than what he can afford? Is he sensible with his money? If all of these things are good, then that's a green flag, because you can tell a lot about the way someone thinks by the way they manage money.

He's a nice guy with an edge

One of the biggest lies told in the world of dating is that nice guys finish last. Guys who are pushovers and doormats (someone you can walk all over) finish last because they don't have that edge to them. But if the man you are dating is a nice guy with an edge, then that's the type of guy you really want to be with.

When I say, 'he has an edge', I mean he will stand up for himself and for those who he loves. He doesn't let anyone step all over him. He will always stand up for what he believes is right. He will display to those closest to him a lot of love; but at the same time he isn't scared to let those who he doesn't like know that he doesn't like them. Basically, a nice guy with an edge is a nice guy with some backbone!

Guys who are nice to everyone, even those who aren't good to them, aren't really just nice guys. They are men who are intimidated of others and want people to like them. A nice guy with an edge is a genuinely nice guy because he won't have an ulterior motive to be nice. He will just be a good guy because that is his true nature.

How he treats the waiter

This is a huge indicator of how somebody really thinks of themselves and others. Always pay attention to how the man you are dating treats those who are in service positions. Is he rude? Does he talk down to those people where they are in positions where they are serving him? Does he have good or bad manners when talking to others that are serving him?

If he is really nice to you, but very rude to people who are serving him, you need to be very careful around this type of person. These types of people are only nice to people who they see as their superiors so they can further elevate their own standing, or they are only nice to people who will give them something that they want but not obligated to (for example, because it's their job). When I say, 'give them something that they want', this could be sex, money, food, entertainment etc. And once this type of person feels like they can no longer benefit from you in some way, they will start being rude to you.

Also, this type of person usually comes with superiority complexes, and if you are in a relationship with them, they will try and assume the dominant positions on everything and won't see you as an equal. It will happen very slowly, and you won't notice it happening until it's too late.

BUT if the man you are dating treats those who are in positions serving him with respect and good manners, it's a green flag. It shows that he doesn't assume that he is better than anyone else and is a much more pleasant type of person.

Think of it like this, if you were the waiter, how would they be talking to you? And would you like how they came across as a person?

He plans dates

This may sound simple and obvious, but it is not to be overlooked. A lot of men will start off the relationship planning dates and making the effort to take you out etc. But, as time goes on, this effort that they make to plan dates happens less and less in a lot of men.

But, if you find a good guy who doesn't stop planning dates with you, then it's a massive green flag. This shows he cares and wants to spend time with you and keep that spark alive in the relationship! I'm not saying that he needs to plan a date every night of the week for you, but once a week is nice. Or if he plans a date one week, then you plan a date the next week, then that's also ok.

However, if you have a man who is ALWAYS planning all of the dates, then you must not get complacent yourself and allow him to make all of the effort planning the dates. I'm a firm believer that it should be a 50/50 effort, otherwise he won't feel appreciated, and it will cause problems in the relationship. So, take it in turns planning the dates and make the effort for each other because it's a great way to keep the spark alive and show appreciation for each other.

How he reacts when you tell him 'No'

You can tell so much about a person and how they see themselves and how they see you when you tell them 'no'.

This is a very big indicator that you must never overlook. If you tell a man 'no' and he reacts aggressively, pushy or anything negative when you're saying 'no', and it is something that is personal about yourself (for example your own body), then that's a major red flag.

Say for example, he wants sex, and you say 'no', and then he gets aggressive; it's showing a huge lack of respect for you, and it shows that he has a superiority complex.

But a green flag is when someone respects you when you tell them 'no'. Again, for example, if you say 'no' to sex, and he is calm and respectful and not pushy about it, then that's great. It shows that he understands your boundaries and respects you. It also shows that he sees you as an equal and not someone who is inferior to him.

At times during life, you will disagree with each other and sometimes you will say 'no', and he will disagree. But a green flag is if he handles it in a calm and respectful way. It also depends on what you're saying 'no' about. If it involves your own body for example, then he must purely respect your 'No'.

Like I said, you can tell a lot about a person by the way they behave when you tell them 'No'.

Good communication

Good communication is one of the main pillars of a healthy relationship. If you don't have good communication in a relationship, then the relationship is always doomed to fail. A big green flag is when someone really takes the time to express their thoughts and feelings to you and someone who takes the time to listen to yours.

If the person you're dating doesn't listen to you, then it's never going to work. Also, if they hide how they are feeling, then that won't work either because it's a pressure build up that's waiting to explode and ultimately destroy the relationship.

Another form of communication that is a must, is that they communicate their schedule with you. That way you can plan dates and other things in life. Also, you'll understand when they are busy, so you won't be worried that they are ghosting you or losing interest in you etc.

So, if you're dating someone and they display good communication (listening, expressing their own thoughts and feelings, telling you their schedule etc), then that's a great green flag! A little communication goes a long way.

He is ambitious

Ambition is a trait that many people find desirable, and for a good reason! The reason why we find ambitious people more attractive comes down to evolutionary psychology. Those who had more ambition throughout time had a better chance at survival. Simple. And it's still hardwired in our brains to find this an attractive trait. But, in this day and age, you don't need to be ambitious to survive. However, again, it's still in us to find this trait desirable in a partner.

But instead, being ambitious serves a different purpose these days instead of simply surviving. If you meet a man who is ambitious, you are meeting a man who wants to grow in life and who will be much more interesting as a person.

An unambitious man will sit on the couch, not push himself, have nothing new to talk about and all the other negative traits that come along with a lack of ambition. But an ambitious man will be active, have lots of new things to talk about, enjoy challenging himself, and want to better your future together.

So, when you are talking to a man on date, pay close attention to whether he comes across as ambitious. Does he want to better himself and his situation? Does he enjoy challenging himself? Does he want to make something of his life? If the answer is yes, it's a fantastic sign. You'll have much more fun with a man who has ambition, as opposed to a man who has none.

He has never cheated

You can tell a lot about a man that you are dating by how he was in his past relationships. For example, does he have a clean past? Or it is littered with marks against his name?

A big green flag is when you find out a man has NEVER cheated in a relationship and has always been loyal. I believe loyalty is very black and white. You either are loyal, or you aren't. There are no grey areas when it comes to loyalty.

You can predict the future of people's behaviours by looking at the patterns of people's pasts. Yes, some people do change, but when it comes to loyalty, it is super rare. So, don't put yourself in a position with somebody where you're hoping that they might change because, 99% of the time, you'll be wasting your own time. Instead, if you find out they haven't been loyal before, run. But, if you find out they have a clean history in relationships of no cheating and 100% loyalty, then that's the type of man you want to be dating!

How to Deal with a Breakup

Many of us handle break ups very differently. Some people like to take their time to heal, which can be very healthy. Others like to jump straight back into the world of dating and meeting new people.

You will get lots of different advice from people, but there are certain suggestions to follow that will help you have a much easier time getting over a relationship and helping you to have the confidence to put yourself back out there.

In this chapter I'm going to give you some tips to help you deal with a breakup...

Level up

After a breakup your confidence might feel at an all-time low. This can be a natural feeling for so many of us after a breakup, especially if we are the person who wasn't the one who ended the relationship; or even when we end a relationship when someone isn't treating us how we deserve to be treated.

When this happens, it can affect your confidence a lot for many different reasons. Such as, we lost a sense of who we really are during the relationship and our confidence that came along with it. But if this is you, fear not. I want you to do this...

FOCUS on levelling up yourself! Really dedicate your time and mind to smashing your own goals.

The gym is your friend in this scenario. Work out to take your mind off the breakup. And when you do this, your body will look better each and every day, and before you know it, you'll be looking hotter than ever.

Dedicate your energy to achieving other goals, such as starting a new business or furthering your career.

Focus on being more social and talking to different people and expanding your social horizons.

Buy yourself new, fashionable clothes. With a new you, you want a new look! Or improve the look you had before. This can be very enjoyable too!

Put all of these things together and you'll feel like a whole new person. Stick to it and you'll realise your own worth because you're actually concentrating on yourself. Then when you look back at your previous relationships, you will see that you are now levels above them. And you'll be wondering what you ever saw in your ex.

Also, you will attract a much higher calibre of partner because you have levelled up yourself.

The funny thing is, when you level up yourself, most

of the time your ex will come running back to you saying that they've made a mistake. DON'T fall for this! Now you're a hotter version of yourself, they will want you. They had their chance. Time to move on to someone more on your own level...

I love seeing someone have a good glow up!

Start dating and meeting new people

One of the biggest hurdles after a breakup is putting yourself back out there to start dating again. Lots of people get very nervous about meeting new people. Sometimes it even feels like you are doing something wrong, like you are cheating on your previous partner, because it's been so long since you have dated other people. Just to clarify, you're doing NOTHING wrong! It's fantastic that you're back out there on the dating scene again.

However, don't rush too quickly into it though if you feel like you have a lot of strong emotions still connected to the old relationship. This is because you won't be fully giving yourself to the dating process. You may also end up projecting old problems from the previous relationship onto the new people that you are dating because you haven't taken the time to heal from the past relationship.

On the other hand, don't leave it too long either because you'll make it a habit to not put yourself out there, and you will turn down dates. And before you know it, you'll be so rusty when it comes to dating, that you'll be a nervous wreck on a date.

The key is finding a healthy balance of not too fast and

not too slow of putting yourself back out there to start dating again.

When you start dating again, you are giving yourself the chance of finding someone new who treats you how you should be treated.

When you do meet the right person, I promise you, you will look back at your previous relationships and wonder why you ever stayed in those relationships.

A new connection with someone who's company that you love being around will make you forget all about your old relationships!

Lessons learnt and bridges burnt

One of the biggest problems people have after breakups is that they hold onto all of the emotions from the previous relationship. I want you to change your mindset when you think about breakups. You need to start seeing them as a lesson. When you do this, you will be able to form much healthier and happier relationships in the future because you will learn of what to do and what not to do when you are with a future partner.

So, let's say for example that you ended a relationship because your partner was being controlling... I want you to look back at those controlling behaviours that they displayed and recognise when they first started. What were the first red flags? How did you react when they showed you these controlling behaviours? Once you identify this, you can learn and grow from it.

For example, let's say you are now talking to or dating someone new. Then they display a red flag such as a controlling behaviour, like your ex did. Now you have two options...

1. Ignore the red flags like you did before and repeat the same type of relationship over again and be miserable in your relationship.

2. Identify the red flags and not talk to that person again, so you don't end up wasting your time on someone who will behave like your ex did.

If you take the 2nd option, you have truly grown as a person. Then when you look back, you will see that the old relationship was just one big lesson to learn from, so you can move into a new relationship with the right person with a healthy understanding of what to do and what to not do.

Lots of people say, 'Don't burn bridges with people, because you never know, one day you might need them in the future'. I MASSIVELY disagree with this. If someone treated you badly in the past, why would you want to stay in contact with them?

Abusive people will try to stay in contact with you, even after you have broken up with them because they like to see you suffer. The best thing you can do with an ex who wasn't nice to you is block them on everything and cut off all contact with them. They served their purpose in your life. And that purpose was that they were a lesson for you to learn. You'll look back in years to come, when you're with your perfect partner, and realise that you're a much wiser person because of it. And because of this you can now help people who are in similar situations as you once were.

How to get over someone

A person who you had strong emotions for can stay in your mind a lot longer than you want them to. You may feel like the emotional attachment is still there with that person. And you may even feel like you're never going to get over them. It could even be that you are anxious about being single and not in a relationship. Change can be scary. But you need to realise that if the person wasn't nice to you, it's not the person that you miss. The thing that you miss is the routine and the known. If you think about it logically, you will never miss someone who didn't treat you right. Your brain is thinking about them because it's what it has known for so long.

To stop thinking about someone, you need to identify when you start to think about them. Is there a trigger? Is there a pattern of behaviour that you do that makes you think of them? Once you recognise this, it's the first step to getting over someone.

Secondly, recognise what the thoughts are that you are having about someone.

When you are trying to get over someone, the thoughts tend to highlight the positive things about that person and not the negative. These bias thoughts are your brain's way of trying to convince you to go back to what it once knew before. Nothing more, nothing less.

But the thing that you need to remember is that the relationship ended for a reason. So, something negative clearly happened. So, when these thoughts come into your head, I want you to pause those thoughts and truly think about the relationship.

Now, I want you to think about all the negative things that person has done to you. Ignore the positives. Only focus on the negatives. Keep repeating this behaviour and eventually you will stop thinking about that person because your brain will start to recognise that flooding you with emotions of missing them and positive thoughts about them won't have you running back to them.

The faster you can do this after a relationship that you left, where someone wasn't treating you right, the better. Leave it too long and the harder it becomes.

Have you ever wondered why people run back to abusive partners? It's because people repeat what they know, and their brain's way of thinking enables this. Don't fall for it. Be strong and remember the negative things that they did to you and know that you deserve someone so much better!

Why you can't stop thinking about him

Even though a man hasn't treated you the right way, he can still get stuck in your head and occupy your thoughts. You may even know that he's a bad person, yet you still feel drawn towards him. Well, I'm going to tell you why that is...

The 1st reason comes down to evolution. When you have sex with someone, your brain is still hardwired to associate sex with pregnancy; even though on a conscious level we know that if you have protection, you can't get pregnant. But your subconscious and biology doesn't know this. Your mind will assume that every time you have sex, you could get pregnant.

So, your brain will pair bond with that man because it will think that you will need to depend upon him to raise children with you. So, your brain will occupy your thoughts with that man so you continue to pair bond with him, so he will help raise your children with you, even though you don't have children with him!

Therefore, if you have sex with a man too soon, you will get the feeling of something we call 'Buyer's remorse'. This is when you feel regret after you have had sex with a man too soon because you haven't got enough information about him yet to decide if he's a high value man who will be a good father; because again, your brain will think you are pregnant because you had sex with him.

So, in a weird way, the reason why you can't stop thinking about him is because it's your brains way of ensuring your unborn, non-existent children's survival!

Now the 2nd reason... This usually comes down to something called 'emotional spiking'. This is when they get your emotions going into states of highs and lows. So basically, when someone is always hot and cold with you, they are using psychology against you.

I want you to think of someone who is a gambler. Gamblers usually don't gamble because of their love for the money. They do it because their brains get addicted to the highs of winning and the lows of losing. This up and down of their emotional state is what gets them addicted to gambling. And it's exactly the same when it comes to some relationships.

Narcissists are particularly excellent at using these tactics of getting people 'addicted' to them by using these emotional highs and lows.

For example, love bombing you at the start by promising you the world and beyond, then being dismissive and acting uninterested in you.

When they are doing this, they are giving you this range of emotions that you associate with them, and it makes you feel more drawn towards them. So, when you and them breakup or are apart, your brain will crave those highs and lows created by the emotions that person invokes in you.

So, your brain then starts thinking about that person because it wants to feed off the emotions that they supplied you with. Even though those lows can feel really low, those highs can feel really high. This is one of the reasons why you see people get back with partners who are no good for them. Basically, they want to feel those highs and lows that only that person can give them. In other words, they are addicted to that person.

Questions to ask yourself to get him out of your head

I'm going to give you three questions to ask yourself to help you put things into perspective and help you get that person out of your head. These questions will help you see things more clearly about how that person treated you and who they really are to you...

Question 1: If you did NOT think that person is good looking, would you be as accepting of their behaviour towards you?

If they answer is no, then that person isn't the person for you. You let your attraction to their looks cloud your judgement of that person and their behaviours towards you. This happens to so many people because they often let their feelings of attraction override the bigger picture. And the bigger picture should be that you want someone who is going to treat you nicely. It's great if you find your partner good looking, but it means nothing if they aren't a good person too.

Question 2: Would you be embarrassed or nervous telling your friends and family how that person treated you?

If they answer is yes, then it shows they treated you very badly. Your partner should never make you feel like this. Your partner should make you feel safe, respected, and secure. For example, if you're nervous to tell your parents about how a man has treated you because you are worried that they won't like him, then you know for a fact that person has treated you badly. Also, you should never feel bad about how someone treats you. It's their fault, not yours.

Question 3: Would you treat someone that you love the same way that they treated you?

If the answer is no, then that person definitely isn't the one for you. You know yourself what is right and wrong and how to treat somebody correctly. If they don't do the same for you and they don't treat you with respect, then don't give that person another thought.

If the person you are thinking about has got any negative answers on these questions, please know that you deserve better, and don't let them occupy your thoughts because they really aren't worth it.

Ghosting

Ghosting is a very common occurrence these days in the world of modern dating. Ghosting is when someone who you are talking to, or dating, just vanishes on you with no explanation.

It can become incredibly frustrating, and it can be very unpredictable. It can make the person who got ghosted question their self-worth, what they did wrong, and what can they do better next time.

But if this is you, don't worry because in this section I'm going to tell you why people ghost others and what you should do if it happens to you. Let's start with why people ghost others...

Why people ghost others

So, let's say you're having a great conversation with someone, you're feeling the good energy, everything clicks between you both, and then they ghost you. It can be incredibly annoying. If this is the case, the majority of the time, it actually had nothing to do with you!

If someone wasn't feeling it with you that's ok, it happens in life. But if they are aware that you like them, instead of just ghosting you, they should at least have the decency to tell you that they are just getting a friend vibe, or something along these lines. That's what someone with good manners would do. But if they don't, here are main reasons why people will ghost others...

1. They just wanted the validation from you. That's right, they just wanted to see if they could have you if they wanted you. Then once they feel they have achieved this strange goal of theirs, they will move on and seek validation from the next person.

2. They are talking to multiple people, and something has progressed further with someone else and everyone else gets dropped.

3. They could be very busy and really wanted to commit to try to date you; but then once their life becomes too busy, they must drop something, and usually it's their dating life.

4. They have inner conflict with themselves. Lots of people have stuff going on in their minds which makes them withdraw and hide themselves away from the world. Unfortunately, everyone else gets left questioning, 'Why did they ghost me?'.

5. They just wanted sex; and because the conversation wasn't going in that direction, then they ghost and move onto the next person to see if they can get sex much easier from them instead.

ALL of these things have NOTHING to do with you! If the conversation is good and you haven't said anything wrong, then the reason why they ghosted you is because of themselves, and you should never let it affect your confidence. Ghosting happens to the very best of us. Sometimes it's something you just can't help. Instead, put that effort and energy into someone who appreciates your time.

Reasons why people come back after ghosting you

It can be one of the strangest things when people come back to you after ghosting you. You may think to yourself, 'Why ghost me if you wanted me all along?'. They often come back giving you excuses why they ghosted you and telling you all the right things that you want to hear; but DON'T fall for it! There are 4 main reasons why people do this, and I'm going to teach you these reasons so you understand what their real motives are...

1. They are bored.

That's right, they just want some company and someone to call or text, so they think, 'Who can I message knowing that they wanted me, so I have someone to talk to... Ah yes... I know...' So, they contact you to entertain themselves.

2. They are seeking validation.

They may be feeling a little low about themselves and need to be validated by others to increase their own self-worth. And because you gave them interest and compliments before, they will contact you to get their fix of validation.

3. Other women reject them so they come back to you

hoping that you will accept them.

All I can say to this is, you are not somebody's 2nd prize, so don't entertain him.

4. They only want sex.

They are sat at home alone and horny and they are thinking, 'Who do I know who liked me before? They might be easy for some quick sex...'. These types of people will turn the conversation sexual very quickly.

To make it simple, if someone has ghosted you before and they try coming back into your life, IGNORE THEM! They always have selfish motives, and you need to protect yourself and not waste the effort that you could be spending on the right person. They have ghosted you once before and I guarantee they will do it again...

Friends and Dating

Your friends can have a very big role to play when you are single and dating. They can be a real strength of yours. But also, some of your friends may have a secret agenda with you. It's important that you learn to recognise what's happening with your friends when dating.

In this chapter I'm going to tell you the things to look out for, what people are really thinking, and the cause and effects that create some of their behaviours. Also, in this chapter it is about your own behaviours in regards to friends and dating. It's an interesting read and I'm sure you'll find it very helpful...

Orbiters

First of all, an 'Orbiter' is somebody who pretends to be your friend, but they secretly want to be with you romantically, but they don't know how to get you attracted to them. They are fake characters and can be very deceitful because they are luring you into a false friendship. And let's be honest, that's creepy.

So many women have these 'Orbiters' around them, and they aren't even aware of it. They think they are friendly guys who have her best interests at heart. You will meet some people who are genuinely nice people who do have your best interests at heart, however, there are many men who pretend to be your friend in order to have sex with you. They are quite easy to recognise once you know what to look out for.

However, I will say this... Someone can be your friend and then it can blossom into something romantic, and that's wonderful. But the difference between that and an 'orbiter' is that an 'Orbiter's' whole game is to PRETEND to be your friend in order to get with you romantically. So, how to identify an 'Orbiter'...

1. Whenever you start talking about other people that you find attractive or you are dating, their behaviour towards you begins to change. Usually, they start acting a bit off and colder towards you.

2. When you put a picture of just yourself on social media, they will like it. But when it's a picture of you and someone you're dating, they will never like it.

3. When you get into a relationship, they become much more distant with you. Or even sometimes angry at you.

4. They will say flirty things to you, and if you don't respond flirtatiously back, they will either say they were just joking to cover up their flirty behaviour towards you, or distance themselves from you and then come back to you after a little bit of time has passed.

5. In conversation they constantly remind you that they are single.

6. They are overly touchy with you.

7. When they do eventually try and make their move on you, and then when you turn them down, they get very angry because they feel very frustrated, because they feel like they have wasted their time in pretending to be your friend.

How you handle an 'Orbiter' is important. Once they have shown you their true agenda of only pretending to be your friend because they want to get with you, you must cut off all contact with that person. I know it may feel hard as you thought they were your friend, but in reality, they weren't.

For example, if an 'Orbiter' flirts with you and gets angry because you didn't give them any romantic interest back, then they distance themselves from you, and then come back to you; then you need to realise they are coming back to you because they find you attractive and want to try again. It has nothing to do with being your friend. Ignore what they say because if they are deceitful enough to pretend to be your friend, they will tell you lies to re-enter your life.

But you now know their true intentions... If you ever did end up in a relationship with one of your 'orbiters', they tend to be very jealous characters and usually have other toxic behaviours. Trust me on this. Be careful of the 'orbiter'. It never ends well...

How to avoid being in the friendzone

Have you ever met someone new in your day-to-day life, perhaps at work, a night out, at the gym or many other places, and you found this person very attractive, yet you end up putting yourself in the friendzone? If it's a yes, don't worry because you're not alone, as so many people are in the same position. It's more common for women to friendzone men, but occasionally men will friendzone women. So, if you feel like this is the case with yourself, I want you to do this...

It's all about being congruent in your behaviours. In other words, you need to be aligned with what you want, how you're saying things, and how you're coming across.

So, when you have met someone new and you think they are attractive, you need stop playing the game in a safe way and display your interest to that person!

My dad had a good saying that I always remembered when growing up, 'Stop playing the game to not lose'. If you play it safe and never take risks, you'll never get what you want. Yes, you won't get flat out rejected playing it safe; but the reason why you aren't getting rejected is because you aren't putting yourself in a position to get rejected by get the man that you want. He can't reject OR accept your flirtations if he doesn't know you are interested in him!

When putting yourself out there in the dating world, the risk of rejection comes hand in hand with the chance of getting what/who you want. So don't let your fear of rejection stop you from having an amazing love life. The feeling of rejection doesn't last long, and you will get over it. The feeling of regret, because you didn't put yourself out there and go for who you want, will last a lifetime.

If you are someone who finds themself in the friendzone more often than not, be sure to take notes. When you meet someone new, be very clear you are not there to be their friend. You're talking to them because you find them attractive. The friendship will grow as you get to know each other. But when you first meet them, you need to make it known that you find them attractive, and you aren't there just to be friends with them.

Start the conversation off as normal, but when you have gotten the pleasantries and light conversations out of the way, start flirting with them. Let your intentions be known.

You could say something as simple as, 'So, have you got a girlfriend?' Something as simple as that will let the man know exactly what's up... That your sexually interested in him.

If he says he does have a girlfriend/wife, then move on. But, if he says no, escalate things...

Say something like, 'That's surprising as you're pretty hot. Don't let it go to your head though.' Deliver this is in a fun, flirtatious way. The ball is then in his court...

See if he gets flustered, starts blushing or gives the same energy back to you, and if he does then that's fantastic. I then want you to end the conversation on a high note...

Take out your phone and say, 'I got to go, but put your number in here, and if you're lucky I might text you.' Again, deliver this in a flirtatious way and I promise you that he will love it, and more importantly you'll never be put in the friendzone!

The sooner you can establish that you aren't there to only be his friend, the better. Do what I said here, and I guarantee he will love it!

How to escape the friendzone

Escaping the friendzone is no easy task, and it will always come at the risk of losing that person as a friend. But if you truly like that person and find them very attractive, I think it is definitely worth the risk, or you'll always be wondering what could have been.

There's two ways of escaping the friendzone. The direct short approach, or the indirect long approach. The choice is yours...

First of all, let's start with the direct short approach... This is where you tell them how you feel. The more honest you are in this approach, the better. Tell them that you have caught feelings for them, how you find them attractive, and would love to try dating them and seeing how it goes. You can do this in person or over text. My only suggestion for this is if you do it in person, make sure that you dress and groom yourself to make yourself look as hot as possible! Then you will have more chance of success. But, be warned, if they don't feel the same, the friendship will never be the same again. This is the risk you must take.

Now the second way of getting out of the friend zone... This approach will take more time, however, ensures a higher chance at success. BUT (and this is a big BUT), because this way will take more time, you run the risk of them dating other people and finding someone else whilst you're executing your plans. Ok, so here it is...

You need to level up and make them see you in a more sexual way; someone that they find very attractive.

Try out a new hotter look with your fashion, get your body into the best shape you can, work on your confidence, make yourself as hot as possible! It will take a bit of time, but at the end of the day he's only human, and he will start to notice that you've become more attractive and are becoming someone who he can see himself with sexually.

Then after you've done this for a while, pay close attention to see whether his behaviour towards you starts to change...

He may start contacting you a little bit more, subtly dropping flirtatious comments into the conversation, you'll notice him checking you out from time to time, he may start trying to break the touch barrier with you more often etc. Either way, if his behaviour starts to change and he's giving you different types of attention, then this is your time to escalate things with him...

Give him the same energy back. Start flirting with him. Also, because he will then be the one initiating the flirting, because you have levelled up and become more attractive, it will be 1000 times easier for you to transition the relationship from friends to lovers, because you have a very low chance of getting rejected from him because he's giving you all the right signals.

He's giving you the embers to build that fire upon. All you must do is keeping adding wood to that fire to set it ablaze. Your relationship will then change from a friendly one to a romantic one.

These are the only two ways out of the friendzone. Best of luck!

How to deal with his friends

The first time you meet his friends can be quite nerve racking, but it doesn't need to be if you know what you're doing. It's important to handle his friends the correct way because a lot of people go to their friends for relationship advice, and they are influenced by their friend's opinions if they are close to them.

The main impression that you want to give off when meeting his friends is to come across as unthreatening and pleasant.

If they are playing games, join them. If they are making jokes, have a laugh with them. Ask them questions and make them feel like you are interested in their lives. They will appreciate this, and whenever the man you are dating brings you up in conversation with them, they will always say positive things about you and see you as a positive person in his life.

But, if you meet one of his friends who you do not like, don't butt heads with them and enter into conflict with them. Instead, just avoid them. Their friend might be the biggest idiot you have ever met and have some not very nice opinions; and if this is the case and they try talking to you, keep everything neutral and don't give them any energy to feed off. Eventually they won't say much else to you, and you haven't affected the dynamics of the group.

However, if they do start being rude directly to you, then you need to observe how the man you are dating, or in a relationship with, behaves. This is all that matters. You shouldn't care what his rude friends think about you. You should only care about how the man you're dating reacts to his rude friends.

So, if his friend is being rude to you, and the man you're dating interjects and defends you, that is a green flag because he can't control his friend's behaviours, but he can control his own actions and react the correct way.

On the other hand, if he doesn't defend you and expects you to have conflict with his friend, that is a huge red flag. You are the one coming into his friendship group. He and his friends should be doing their best to make you feel safe and welcome.

If he won't stand up for you, he will forever be a weak partner and he clearly lacks social etiquette. That's not the type of man you want to be with.

After this has happened and he hasn't defended you, then give him only one chance (assuming it wasn't anything completely out of order or offensive) and tell him how it made you feel. If he then corrects it IMMEDIATELY and has a talk with his friend and says not to do it again, then that is ok and let him off...

But he should only be needed to be told this ONCE because he may have been unsure of what to do the first time it happened. It's still not excusable but give him one chance to redeem himself because he may be a little unsure of how to handle the situation.

However, if he doesn't correct it at all (or interject immediately without you needing to tell him to if his friend has said something VERY offensive to you), then leave him, because he clearly doesn't respect you enough to interject when someone is being rude to you. And in my opinion, that is a very weak, low value man.

This isn't a matter of whether you can stand up for yourself or not; and if you really want to give his rude friend a piece of your mind, by all means gives go for it; however, I think it's the perfect opportunity to see what the man you are dating is really like in these scenarios. The rude friend is just a tool in this test to see whether the man you are dating behaves correctly. It's about seeing if the man you have chosen to date, or be in a relationship with, respects you enough to stand up for you when you are coming into his social circle, so you feel welcome, safe and respected.

Is my friend jealous of my new relationship?

Here is something that doesn't get talked about enough in the world of dating. Some friends will become very jealous when you start dating someone who is high value.

Lots of our friends have our best interests at heart, and true friends will be thrilled that you have found someone you are happy with. But some other 'friends' won't be so happy. There are a few reasons why, and they all come from a selfish place...

The 1st reason is because they wish they have what you have. So, instead of being happy for you when you tell them about the new person in your life, they will pick fault at every little thing about them, even when there is nothing to fault. They will always put a negative spin on things. Jealousy makes people act in very strange ways and I've seen this happen so many times. It mainly stems from their own frustrations because they can't attain what you have attained. This type of person is never a true friend. They are someone that you need to be very cautious around.

The 2nd reason is because you will be spending less time with them. They got used to you always being around them because you were single and had more free time. So instead, they will try and make you feel guilty for not spending as much time with them, instead of themselves going out there and finding someone for themselves. As long as you still make time for your friends, that is all that matters. They can't expect you to be joined at the hip with them for the rest of their lives!

And the 3rd reason is because the feel possessive over you. This is a very toxic type of friendship where they see you as a possession in their lives. They see you as someone who isn't an individual with their own story, but a character in theirs. They will be rude and hostile towards your new partner even when your partner is polite to your friend.

If you see your friend acting in any of these jealous ways, talk to them about it and tell them how it makes you feel. If they correct their behaviour, that's great! If they don't, perhaps they were never your friend to begin with. You were just someone who was convenient to them when they needed you around. True friends won't exhibit any of these traits towards you and will be thrilled for you that you have found someone you are happy with.

The art of being a good wingwoman/wingman

Having a good wingwoman/wingman is a God send in social situations. They can really elevate your chances of getting someone attracted to you, and set the right environment for you and the person you like to build attraction with each other.

Lots of people claim they are a good wing, but in my whole life I can count on one hand the amount of truly good wings I have met and witnessed. It's a skill that takes an intelligent person to be able to pull off correctly. So, in this section I'm going to give you some simple tips on how to be the best wingwomen/wingman you can be!

1. Your wingwomen/wingman needs to understand that they represent your value by association.

If your wing is acting unclassy and low value in front of the person you are trying to attract, then it makes you look bad as well. But, if your wing comes across as someone who is classy and high value in front of the person you find attractive, then they will also think that you are classy and high value too. Birds of a feather flock together.

2. The wing must never outshine the person they are winging.

When you are in a group and having a conversation, the wing must come across as someone who is chatty, classy, friendly, and nice... but never outshine the person they are winging. If they feel like more of the attention is on them, they need to hold back and allow you to talk and give you a chance to display higher value. They must also NEVER interrupt you because it will make you seem as a lower value person in the group.

3. They need to create a situation where you can be alone with the person you find attractive.

Let's say there are 4 of you. 2 women and 2 men, and you find one of the men attractive, and your wing knows who that is; then they need to get you in a situation alone with the person you find attractive. For example, your wing could say to the man's friend, 'I'm going to the bar to get a drink. Can you please come with me, so I don't have to carry everything alone.' Then once they go, you and the person you find attractive are alone together.

4. Your wing needs to handle interference.

So, let's say your wing has successfully got you and the person you think is attractive alone together... then other people keep trying to join the conversation you are having. A good wing will see this happening, then come into the conversation and start a conversation with the person who is interrupting you. And then that allows you to take the person you think is attractive somewhere else with you, so you are alone together again.

5. And this is an important rule for yourself...

You must do exactly the same for your wing when they need one! Being a wing and having a wing is something that needs to be built on trust and teamwork. If both of you give it your best, you will have amazing results on a night out together!

Social Dynamics

Having an understanding of social dynamics is a HUGE eye opener. You'll start seeing things other people don't see. You'll start understanding things that others don't. You'll understand why people are attracted to others; and why people react in certain ways to different situations in a social environment.

Everybody is different, yet we all share so many similarities; and once you understand how someone thinks, you can really use it to your advantage.

Ok, so I'm going to give you some tips and knowledge on understanding the social dynamics that applies to dating. Let's get into it...

Frames

Frames are what holds EVERYTHING together in social situations. The easiest way to define social frames are how people function in their culture, family, friend interactions, workplace, social groups, as an individual, and pretty much anything that involves social aspects.

Everything is interlinked. Framework is the web that holds everything together. I'm going to keep everything as easy as possible to understand and relate it to your dating and relationship life, otherwise this could be another book within itself.

Ok, when you are dating you always want to have the stronger, or equal frame to the person you want to attract.

You can come across as needy and desperate if you're coming from a weaker frame compared to the other person. An example of coming from a weaker frame and the other person losing attraction for you would be this...

Let's say you are texting someone and they take hours to reply to you, but every time they do reply to your text, you instantly text them back. You are then coming from a weaker frame.

Another example is if you are talking to someone and you ask them a question; for example, you say to them, 'How was your day?' and they say, 'Good' and nothing else. Then you ask them another question saying, 'How was your work?' and they say, 'Ok'. Then you keep asking them questions and they aren't doing the same back to you, then you are coming from a weaker frame.

This is because you are putting in more effort and seeking value from that person when they aren't doing the same to you. If you do this you will be coming across as lower value than them, and they will lose attraction for you.

We will keep it simple...When talking to people, think to yourself, 'Am I putting in more effort than this person?'. If the answer is yes, then you are coming from a weaker frame.

Another way to either come from a stronger or weaker frame is with your body language...

If you are sat down leaning froward in a conversation (pecking), and they are leaning back, they will notice this, or at the very least subconsciously pick up on this, and you'll be in the weaker frame. But if you lean back and they lean into you when talking, then you control the frame, and they will perceive you as more attractive. If you both lean back, or both lean forward, you are on an equal frame which is also great.

The goal is to be in a stronger or equal frame. NEVER come from the weaker frame when trying to build attraction. It's good to know how this works because this is the foundation of a lot of attraction building.

High Value Women and Dating

This may sound a bit strange but being a high value woman can make dating VERY difficult. When I say a high value woman, I'm talking about women with traits such as good morals, intelligence, kindness, ambition, takes care of her appearance, takes care of her physical and mental health to the best of her ability, loyal, and all other great traits.

The unfortunate thing about men is that so many of them have big egos and get threatened when a woman of high value comes along. Two things happen with these types of men...

1. They avoid her all together because being around her makes them feel inferior and it makes them feel insecure

about themselves.

2. They start dating her, and slowly over time, they chip away at her confidence and belittle her to make her self-esteem go down. These are narcissists and they are very calculated at doing this. It's called 'poison dripping'. It happens over a long period of time, little by little, and she doesn't notice what's happening until it's too late. Then you see a high value woman, who has so much to offer, suffer from a lack of confidence and she never saw it coming.

Men who are intimidated by and/or belittle women's achievements are weak men who you NEVER want to date. One of the saddest things I see as a dating coach is when a high value woman suppresses her achievements and worth to attract more men by trying to come across as less intimidating in the man's eyes. NEVER do this! You'll end up with a man who isn't right for you.

That's why you should ONLY date high value confident men because they will love your achievements and strong traits, and your relationship will be much happier and healthier because of his mentality.

Society puts a lot of pressure on men to be the best at everything, and a lot of men fall into this way of thinking, even when it comes down to their own partner. When they get intimidated by/jealous of their partner because their partner is doing better than them... well, they don't want a partner who they see as an equal, they want someone that they feel superior too. And honestly, these types of men are pathetic and not worth your time.

Don't let anyone dim your light! The right man will love you at your very best!

A high value man WANTS a high value woman. And this is why you MUST only date high value men!

Meet interest with interest and disinterest with disinterest

This is a very important lesson to learn when dating and be sure to always keep it in your mind...

It's simple... Meet their interest with your own interest and meet their disinterest with your own disinterest.

One thing our brains are usually good at is recognising patterns. If we do something nice for someone and we get rewarded in return, then they are going to do that nice thing again. If we do something bad, then we get punished for it, we won't do that thing again. This also applies to dating and relationships!

One of the biggest mistakes people make when dating is, when someone pulls away from them, they try harder to be nicer to them, hoping that it will stop the other person from pulling away. But it never works.

So, let's say that you treat your partner very nicely and then they stop making as much effort with you overall, and you start thinking to yourself, 'I need to try harder, then they will like me more' and then you start putting in more effort... When you do this, they will keep pulling away from you and lose attraction for you.

This is because you are rewarding that person for pulling away from you; so they will keep repeating that behaviour over and over again because you always try harder with them when they pull away from you.

It's a low value behaviour and you will fall entirely into their frame. Even though you're being a nice person, unfortunately that's how people's brains are hardwired to think.

So, you may be asking, 'What do I do if someone is pulling away from me and how do I get them back?' It's actually much simpler than you may think...

If someone is pulling away from you, show them disinterest.

If you usually compliment them a lot, stop giving them compliments. If you usually give them a lot of physical affection, display dismissive body language to them instead. They will start to feel this behaviour you're displaying to them and recognise the patterns that when they don't behave in a nice manner to you, they won't get any interest from you. Watch how their behaviour changes and watch them stop repeating negative behaviours towards you.

There does come a point though, that when you do this to them and they don't change, end the relationship because they aren't ignorant of their behaviour, they simply want to be single.

On the other hand, give your interest to those who show interest back to you. This is how healthy relationships happen.

For example, if they make an effort planning a date with you, then you plan the next one. Take it in turns showing affection to each other, and before you know it, it will be normal behaviour to be kind and show interest to each other. This applies to most areas of dating and relationships.

One of the simplest ways of putting it is like this... If a dog bites you and you give it a treat, the dog will bite you again (meeting bad behaviour with interest and reward). But, if you punish the dog for biting you and don't give it attention for a little while after it has bitten you (meeting bad behaviour with disinterest), it won't bite you again and will be nicer to you the next time. People work in exactly the same way!

The Buyer-Seller mentality

This is a golden tip that will definitely make you more relaxed and enjoy dating more, and you will come across as more attractive at the same time.

A lot of people go into the world of dating hoping that people will like them and get worried about what people think of them. Naturally we want people to like us, but if we make that too obvious to somebody that we want them to really like us, and seek their approval and validation, we will be lowering our value to that person, and they will lose attraction for us.

So, having a SELLERS mentality is basically where you are trying to sell yourself to that person. You'll be showing signs that you really want validation from that person; and as soon as they see this behaviour from you, they will lose attraction for you.

A few examples of this are...

When someone brags about themselves to try and impress the other person.

Always making themselves available for the other person, even at their own inconvenience.

Putting more effort into the relationship than they receive, hoping that it will make the other person like them more.

They will pick up on these signals that you're giving off and it will make them think, 'Why are they trying to convince me to like them?' or 'Why are they coming across as so needy?' It will be a big turn off for them because it will come across as though the other person is a higher value than yourself. So, instead do this...

Every time you go on a date with someone, or just having a conversation, I want you to change your mentality to the BUYER mentality.

Say to yourself, 'Let's see if I like this person' or, 'What does this person bring to the table that I like? Are they a good conversation? Do I find them attractive? Do their morals match up with mine?'

When you go into new interactions with people NOT trying to sell yourself, but instead having the mentality of, 'Let's see if I like this person', you will be giving off energy and behaviours that are much stronger and more high value, and the other person will feel that.

And again remember, men like the chase. If they think you're going to be an easy ride for them because you sell yourself to them (metaphorically of course), then they will lose interest in you.

Also, when you have the buyer's mentality and start focusing on what other people bring to the table, you won't ignore their red flags if they do have any because you'll be more focused on if you like them, instead of if they like you.

Think of it like this... When you go to buy a car, who

has the power? The person buying the car or the person selling the car? It's the buyer because the car salesperson wants and needs to sell you something, and because of this they can become quite annoying! It's exactly the same when dating.

I urge you to have this buyer's mentality as it is a game changer when you are dating, and you'll be much more likely to meet the person who is right for you!

Who does he surround himself with?

This is a very important question to ask yourself when you are dating someone. You can tell a lot about a person by the company that they keep.

They say that you are the 5 people you spend the most time with. I believe there is an element of truth to this statement, however, we are all individuals with our own interests and unique experiences; but who we chose to spend our time with is a choice that we willingly make by ourselves. Remember this saying, 'Birds of a feather flock together'.

So, how does this apply to the man that you're dating? Let's start off with the glaring red flags...

If he surrounds himself with other men who cheat on their girlfriends and spends time with them and laughs and finds commonalities with these types of men, then it's a very bad sign.

First of all, he's going to be more exposed to negative influences. Secondly, he clearly doesn't think it's such a bad thing to be in the company of men who are unfaithful to their partners behind their backs. Thirdly, it shows that his choice in friends is those of low quality. This could show that he may be scared of confrontation with his friends (not saying to them what they are doing is wrong), and/or it shows that someone having good morals doesn't matter to him when picking his friends. All of these are very undesirable traits that you don't want to have in a partner.

On the other hand, you can usually tell if he is going to be a good person by the company that he chooses to have around him.

If the people he willingly spends his time with have great morals, treat their partners with respect and are overall good characters, then it's a great sign. It means he actively chooses to be around positive influences. If all of his friends are great boyfriends and husbands, chances are he will be too.

Is age just a number?

I get asked this question a lot. Many people find themselves finding somebody who is much older or younger than themselves very attractive, and they are unsure of whether to pursue that person or not. There are a few factors that are important to remember when it comes to age differences and dating. First of all, this applies to everyone who is over the age of 18! Let's get into it...

The first factor that you need to look at is... Do you want children? Do they want children? If your answers don't align with what yours and their goals are on this first question, then the relationship is very unlikely to work.

When there is an age gap, the question of having children needs to be answered. You may really like someone older than you, but if they don't want to have children and you do, or vice versa, it's not going to work.

Something that a lot of people think of is that age = maturity. That 100% is not true.

I've met many people who are older but very immature, and I've met people who are younger and very mature. And of course, I've met immature younger people and mature older people. It all comes down to the individual. Their life experiences, their natural temperament, their upbringing, different life references that they refer to, and many more reasons.

So, let's say you are a lady who is 40 years old, and you meet a man who is 30 years old. The first thought running through many women's heads are, 'This guy won't be mature enough for me.'... This is not always true though. If this is you, please don't miss the opportunity of getting to know someone because they are younger than you, because that person may surprise you in a good way.

Another question to ask yourself is... 'Do our life goals add up and do we want the same thing?'

People who are at a younger age tend to be a bit more fluid and flexible with their life goals because they change as they grow up into someone entirely different. Whereas someone who is a bit older will have experienced more and will be firmer in what their life goals are.

So, for example, let's say the younger person wants to travel the world, and so does the person who is older. That's great. But the younger person is more likely to then change what their life goals are over time. For example, they might want to settle down, buy a house and establish themselves in their career. Whereas the older person still wants to continue travelling because they have done all of these other things before. It's something to think about when there's an age gap in a relationship. The longevity of each other's life goals, and if the life goals align.

Another factor about dating somebody with a big age gap is that many people are worried about getting judged by others.

They may have met someone who is perfect for them, however, because there's an age gap, they don't pursue it because they are worried about what their friends, family and other people may think. Because it's not considered 'normal' by society, people feel judged and don't pursue things that aren't considered as 'normal' because that's the way most people are socially conditioned to think throughout their whole life.

I think that if you like someone and there is an age gap, that you should ignore everyone's opinions about your relationship. As long as you are happy and good to each other then it is no one's business about the age difference in your relationship. If your friends and family don't support it, even though your partner treats you perfectly, then they clearly are very immature people and don't have your best interests at heart. They are clearly more concerned about what others may think. Again, ignore these people. As long as you are both happy, that is all that matters.

In my opinion, when it comes to age gaps in relationships, I think that you need to do exactly what makes YOU happy. If you have an amazing connection with someone and your goals align and they treat you correctly, then you'd be very silly to not date them because of something like an age gap. If you don't date them then you may then be searching your whole life to find someone who you share as strong a connection with as that person, and you may never find it. Sometimes you need to ignore everyone and do exactly what makes you happy.

Religion, politics, and cultural differences when dating

Religion, politics and cultural differences is something that you must learn how to navigate when dating. In an ideal world it would all be extremely easy, and these things wouldn't be an issue, but unfortunately that is not always the case. With some people it is an issue, but with others it is not.

So, I'm going to break down each topic for you and what I think you would need to do in order to navigate these topics and give you a better chance of success when dating.

Religion

Religion is something that can make or break a relationship for a lot of people. People have different views of how to live their lives according to religion. It is important to find out people's religion when dating them and how strong their views are. For example, some people are religious but aren't very strict on the rules within that religion but they still like what that religion embodies, and they want to follow certain practices of that religion. However, some people may strictly follow the rules of a religion and it could become a barrier in pursuing a relationship with them.

Just to clarify, there is no right or wrong answers when it comes to religion. It's all about what you want in a partner and whether your own religion, or theirs, will be able to make that possible.

A big example is that many religions have rules of no sex before marriage. Whereas to some people, sex is a very important part of a relationship before marriage. So, 99% of the time, if two people have opposing rules on this, then they aren't going to be compatible in a relationship together.

Another big factor about religion when dating is that both people must fully respect what the other person's religious choices are, never force their religion upon the other person, or critique the other person's religion in a negative manner.

Also, when dating somebody who follows a different religion to you, it is important to see if the religion's morals align with your own morals. And if they don't, then how much are you willing to look the other way? Is it a deal breaker for you? Will they have certain expectations of you if you date them? These are serious questions to ask yourself when dating someone from a different religion.

In my opinion I believe that people from different religions can definitely work well in a relationship together. However, the biggest factor in my mind to making it work is respecting each other's religious views.

Political views

Ah politics... This is always a sensitive topic for many people when dating and in relationships.

In a world that is becoming more politically unpredictable with politics always in the headlines because of the way the world is, knowing your partner's political views is important. It all depends on whether your views are on the right, the left, a bit of both, or something completely different, how strong your views are, and how tolerant you are of other people's views.

I feel like to ask someone's political views early on when dating them is a bit of a strange thing to do. But what I have found is that if someone has very strong political views, they will usually make it known quite early on when dating them.

If you share the same views, then great! If you don't, then you may want to reconsider if that person is for you. It can lead to many arguments. But what I have found is that two people can have different political views and get along very well. It all depends on how you both discuss your different views with each other.

When you are discussing differences in opinions, is the conversation respectful to each other? Do they get angry when you don't agree with them? Do they force their political views on to you? These are important observations you must make.

Some of my best friends have very different views to me, but I still think of them as my best friends because they are respectful to me, and I am respectful to them. And in a relationship, if you and your partner do everything the correct way, then it can still be a happy relationship if you have different political views. However, if you feel like their political views are something that you can't overlook, then it's best to not date that person.

Cultural differences

Cultural differences can be an amazing thing when dating. You can learn so much from somebody who has a different cultural background to you. Such as, different music, customs, food etc. You'll be sucked into a world that you would have never experienced unless you met that person.

Many people don't date people outside of their culture because they don't understand it. This is because people tend to stick to what they know because they are worried to have new experiences, and then miss out on different things in life.

I say fully embrace dating people from different cultures! You'll find this very exciting because you'll have new experiences that you wouldn't have had before meeting someone from a different culture. Also, you'll have more things to talk about because you'll always be learning and doing new things.

However, I will give this piece of advice... Don't force your culture upon someone you are dating. Respect their choices if they don't want to do something that they aren't comfortable with. It's all about respecting each other. If you can do that, I guarantee that you will have some amazing experiences with each other and discover new things that you will end up loving. And it's all because you started dating someone who is from a different cultural background to you.

Money and jobs when dating

Money and jobs when dating is always a topic that is heavily discussed. Many people have different views on this topic. But isn't all black and white; there are some grey areas in it too, and it really does come down to the individual. There are a few things to break down when it comes to money and jobs when dating, so here they are...

Expectations people face

Today, unfortunately, we live in a society where many people link their own value to what job they have or how much money they have in the bank. This is particularly more prominent in men than it is in women.

Many men feel that in order to get a high value woman, he needs to have an amazing job, or lots of money in the bank. And this really is not the case, but it's the reality he creates in his head.

In my personal experience as a dating coach for quite some time, with the 1000's of women I have spoken to, I genuinely can't remember even 10 women saying to me that it matters if a guy makes a lot of money.

The only thing most women care about (and I agree with this) is that the man can pay his own way, he doesn't rely upon his partner to pay his bills or to pay for his share of the dates etc, he is financially stable, and he is able to provide a comfortable life if they have a family. That's all 99% of women ask for, and I believe that is the correct way of thinking.

However, unfortunately, in the media, the general consensus says that a man must have a lot of money to be considered a high value man. It's very sad to see and a very immature outlook on life.

On the other hand, the culture of dating is a little different when women have a lot of money. Many men, due to this societal pressure, feel emasculated when dating a woman who earns more than him. This is because of the societal pressure placed upon him to be the 'bread winner' of the family, and in his head, it means that she has more worth than he does because she has more money than him.

If you are ever in a position where a man feels emasculated because you earn more than him, get rid of him and leave him instantly. These types of men will try to belittle you in other areas of your life to compensate for their lack of money and how they link it to their own self-worth. These types of men will try to drag you down to what they perceive as a lower level of worth than themselves. It's a very sad thing to see and it's something that you don't need in your life. Your partner should be thrilled that you're doing so good financially. You're a team, where it's you two vs the world. Not against each other!

Also, something else I do come across very often is when a woman earns a lot of money, she will often downplay and hide the fact that she has a lot of money. This is because she is scared of making a man feel emasculated, and she is scared of scaring away potential suitors.

It's a real shame to see when a woman has this mentality, because when she does this, she isn't being her authentic self. Because of this she is only going to attract men who have false perceptions of her lifestyle.

Some men might find out later on that she earns more than them and it may intimidate them. Or some men might find out later on that she earns a lot of money and genuinely not care that she has a lot of money because they are secure within themselves. But they may be thinking that she has a secret agenda if she is hiding the fact that she has a good job and earns a lot. He may think that she thinks that he isn't going to like her for her, and then assume that she is a bit of a liar, and it may scare him away.

Instead, if she didn't hide what she did for a living, then she will stop the insecure men coming forward and wasting her time. But the genuinely secure and confident men will think that it is an accolade and want to get to know her for her.

<u>People and their jobs and how it crosses over into the world of dating</u>

It's ok to find certain jobs attractive. It's also ok to find other jobs unattractive. You can tell a lot about someone by the job that they do. Their levels of ambition, contentment in what they do, their ethics and morals, their understanding of how diverse the world really is, and much more. However, that isn't always the case for everyone because different circumstances produce different outcomes on what jobs people do and their perspectives on jobs.

It is also very interesting to see what someone thinks of your job when you tell them what you do for a living, and you can tell a lot about someone by the way they react when you tell them about your job.

So, I'm going to break this topic down into different

sections...

<u>It's the traits they possess that got them the job that's attractive</u>

When dating it's very important to not get sucked into what jobs society finds attractive. Instead, you should be looking for the attractive traits that got them to where they are in their career. Ambition, discipline, intelligence, caring, likeability, etc. So, when you are dating, I want you to do this...

Do not turn people away or make assumptions of people based on what they do for a job. (Unless it's a job you despise because it conflicts with your own moral compass). Instead take your time getting to know someone. Listen to what they are saying. Is it filled with all the desirable traits that you find attractive, such as ambition and intelligence? Do they have certain goals in their life they want to achieve? Do they seem like a character who will do everything in their power to make their dreams a reality? That is all that truly matters.

It doesn't matter what someone does for work (as long as they can pay for themselves, and they have the desire to progress in their own career). What matters is if they have the character traits to better their life and those of their loved ones. If they do have the desirable traits that will help you build a happy, stable future together, then that is what is important. Also, it's a huge flex to be the woman who was with him from the start instead of the woman who came along when he had everything.

What I'm saying is, don't go for someone based on what they are currently doing for work. Instead, go for them on the traits that will make them successful in their career. Mix these traits in with a man with a good moral compass, loving characteristics, healthy mindset etc, and you've got yourself an amazing catch!

Sub-Dom dynamics and jobs

Just to clarify: This does not apply to everyone, but this is the general consensus for the majority of people... You can usually tell how someone will be sexually and in a relationship by what job they do.

Usually if someone is in a dominant position in the workplace, 9/10 times they like to be submissive in a relationship.

For example, if someone is a CEO of a company and they are constantly telling people what to do all day every day, then in their romantic relationships they prefer the complete opposite. They usually become very submissive in their relationships.

It's our brains way of balancing everything out. That's why you see a lot of these high-end businessmen, who are very dominant in their workplace, who are very submissive sexually. It's the usually same for women too. The majority of women who are dominant in the workplace love having a dominant partner so they can feel more feminine at home.

These sub-dom dynamics don't always come out in the day-to-day life of a relationship, but during sex when the psychological filters aren't as strong, then that's when these sub-dom dynamics come out more; and again, it's usually the opposite of how they feel in their day-to-day life.

So, pay attention to what someone does for work, and it will give you a window into whether they like to be more submissive or dominant in their relationship and sex life.

Words of Wisdom from your Dating Coach

In this chapter I'm going to give you some words of wisdom to help you your love life.

These words of wisdom will hopefully make you think more deeply about the type of people that you're dating, in a relationship with, or people you are going to date.

I have personally found these quotes and ways of thinking very beneficial to my mindset throughout my entire life, and I have no doubt that you will also find them as helpful as I have. I know you'll then have these thoughts and quotes with you for the rest of your life. Let's get into it...

You buy cheap, you buy twice

This is a quote that my father has always said to me growing up, 'You buy cheap, you buy twice'. This 100% applies to your love life too. Of course, we don't buy people! But it's a perfect analogy for how to view your dating life and your relationships.

One of the most criminal things you can do to yourself is simply settling for someone because you can't find someone else who you think is the full package. When you do this, you will end up resenting the relationship you are in, not feeling attracted to them, perhaps they won't treat you right, you don't enjoy their company, or a thousand other reasons why simply settling for someone who you aren't attracted to is such a bad thing.

Either way, you have ultimately wasted your time on this person who wasn't good for you, and you will have to put yourself back out there in the world of dating and look for someone new to date again.

But if you take your time and date people who you genuinely see as someone who is a good for you instead of rushing things with the wrong person, then you won't need to keep re-entering the world of dating.

When you are dating you only need to find the person who is right for you ONCE! Find that one person who is perfect for you, and you won't need to put yourself back out there again.

So, I'll say it again, 'You buy cheap, you buy twice'. You're a woman who wants a high value man. Correct? So don't waste your time on low value men.

See things for what they truly are

We all want to find love, have the perfect partner, and have the perfect relationship. And I genuinely think that having clear goals of what you want in a relationship and from a partner is a great thing to have. But it's very important that you don't create a fake narrative of what is actually happening when you are dating someone, or in a relationship with someone, because you want to live this perfect life.

When people do this they tend to make excuses for people's bad behaviours because they are so fixated on making their dream situation a reality. This particularly happens when someone feels like they are getting too old to find someone new. (Sidenote: You're NEVER too old to find someone new).

So, what happens is, people will ignore a lot more red flags than they should because they think they can see the potential in a person and the relationship. Which brings me to my next point...

In many cases, going after somebody because you see they have potential is a one-way ticket to a failed relationship. You're falling for somebody who doesn't exist yet. Then you will get your expectations up, and then frustrations arise because they aren't turning out the way you expected them too.

It's also not fair on them if you fall for who they could become, because if they don't become that person it's not their fault and they will be confused as to why there are frustrations arising from you.

So, if you're looking for the full package in someone, (which is what you should always be doing), keep it at that and only date people who you see a genuine future with, just the way they are now.

See things, relationships, and people for who they are. Not what and who they could be...

Right package, wrong address

I've seen this happen so many times. People get into relationships and then it doesn't work out, and then they start questioning themselves with thoughts like, 'What's wrong with me?', 'Am I the problem?', 'I don't think I did anything wrong, so why did they leave me?'

Sometimes, you didn't do anything wrong! You could be the most perfect partner ever, but if the person you're with isn't the right person for you, it just won't work.

I've met so many people who have had failed relationships where I can genuinely say that they are great catches and have done nothing wrong. But because things didn't work out for them, their confidence takes a hit, and their self-esteem goes down. But it doesn't need to...

Sometimes it's because the other person doesn't know how to be in a healthy relationship, sometimes it could be that lifestyles clash, sometimes the other person just turns out to be a bad person, sometimes people just aren't right for each other, and there are many more other reasons.

But it doesn't mean that you're not the perfect partner. You are the full package. You just haven't been delivered to the right address yet.

When choosing between two people, always choose the 2nd one

I've often been asked, 'I like two people, but I don't know who to go for. What should I do?'

It's actually a very simple question to answer. Always pick the person you liked 2nd. This is because if you really liked the 1st person, you wouldn't have liked the 2nd person.

When you really like someone, you will not have eyes for anyone else. You will be fixated upon that one person. That's why I believe that if someone has cheated on their partner, they never truly loved their partner. Even if they tell me that they love them, but they cheated on them, I will tell them that they didn't truly love them.

Let's use an example from the early stages of dating someone… For example, you have been on 3 dates with a man, and then a new man starts talking to you and you really want to date the new man…

Then you should always date the new man and stop dating the 1st man…

Because if you wanted to date the new man but stopped yourself from doing it, you wouldn't be fully satisfied with the relationship with the 1st man if it did ever get to the girlfriend/boyfriend stage. This is because you'll always be wondering, 'What if…?'

When you meet the right person for you, you won't have any interest in dating other people. So, if you must pick between two people, always pick the person you liked 2nd.

People will treat you how you let them

Unfortunately, the world isn't all sunshine and rainbows. There are many people out there who will take advantage of nice people.

I am very sure that if you're someone who is a nice person, people would have tried taking advantage of you at some point in your life. Or perhaps you're a person who isn't very good at setting clear boundaries, then you would have come across many people who will push your limits all the time.

I always believe the saying, 'Give people an inch and they will take a mile'. Of course, this doesn't apply to everyone because there are good people out there, but when dating you need to be careful or people will take advantage of you. People will 100% treat you the way you let them.

So, when dating be very clear about what your boundaries are. And if they try overstepping your boundaries, then leave them and the situation.

The minute you start letting things slide, is the minute people will start thinking that they can get away with a lot more than they should be thinking.

Set your boundaries, don't tolerate disrespect, and leave situations where you feel people aren't treating you correctly, and you will have a much more enjoyable dating experience.

You are the main character in your love story

I love giving people this tip... You are the main character in your love story. You really are!

So many people try changing who they are, so they fit into somebody else's love story. They lose their own identity in the pursuit of someone else, and think they need to behave in a certain way in order to make everyone like them. But I'm telling you that it's ok if not everyone likes you. If everyone liked you then you're doing something wrong. It means you aren't going after what you want and being your authentic self. You're changing who you are to fit into their love story. In other words... people pleasing.

People pleasing comes from a place of anxiety. There are many different reasons for people pleasing, but the most common one is because you're worried about people liking you which could trigger feelings from the past where others didn't like you and it affected your self-esteem. You want others to like you and you try to control the situation, so you don't have those feelings again.

When in reality, when you are people pleasing, you are actually hurting yourself because you aren't going for what you want and being your authentic self. Because of this you are always in a state of anxiety, you will become needy a lot of the time, and overall, you will never be happy coming from a place where you are always people pleasing.

So, I want you to start seeing yourself as the main character of your love story. Every interaction you go into when dating, I want you to stop thinking, 'I hope this person likes me', and start thinking, 'Do I like this person?'.

It's ok to not see someone again. It's ok if you don't like someone and they don't like you. It's ok to be a bit selfish when you are single and pursue what makes you happy.

After all, you're the main character of your own life and you need to do what makes you happy.

If you aren't somebody's first choice, remove yourself so you aren't a choice

Have you ever dated someone and found out that they are struggling to choose between you and somebody else? Well, if this is happening to you, you only have one option... If you aren't their first choice, remove yourself so you aren't a choice.

Do you really want to be competing with someone else for a man's attention and affections? I hope not.

Let's say you did continue to date this man for a while, and they were also dating another person at the same time because they can't make their mind up about who they want.... Well, I 100% believe they have made their decision. They want to have both women at the same time because they are being greedy and want to get the benefits of dating the both of you (or even more people than just the two of you).

It's ok if it's very early days and you are in the talking stage, and they are talking to other people. It happens and it is perfectly normal. But if you've been on a few dates together and they still can't decide if they want you or another woman, remove yourself from the situation because those scenarios never end well. Plus, you'll always be wondering if he ever thinks about the other woman and if he still likes her, and that is not good for your mental health or your relationship.

So, if you're not somebody's first choice, remove yourself so you're not a choice!

Trust your gut instinct

When dating you should always trust your instincts. They are usually correct. If you feel like something is off, then it probably is. If you feel like it's the right time to make a move, then it very well could be. If you feel like someone is flirting with you, trust your instincts and flirt back. Our instincts and gut feelings that we have about scenarios aren't unfounded and random. They are happening to us for a reason, and this why...

Our brains are always working for us even when we aren't aware of it. Our subconscious is always looking out for things and picking up details that our conscious minds tend to ignore.

For example, if you're talking to someone and you're getting a specific energy from them, such as, they are flirting with you, concealing their true intentions, telling you the truth, being deceitful etc, then it's happening for a reason...

Our instincts are just our subconscious picking up on very small details our conscious minds haven't. And it manifests itself into this feeling that we have, which we call our instincts.

Perhaps your subconscious picked up on a slight change of pitch in their voice tonality, or a piece of body language they did, or our subconscious has picked up on some small details of a story and put two and two together and worked out the real reason why someone has done something.

All of these examples, and more, are things that our conscious minds could have missed. So, never ignore your instincts!

How to keep the spark alive

One of the most common questions I get asked as a dating and relationship coach is, 'How do I keep the spark alive?' It's much easier than you may think...

The biggest thing a lot of people don't realise is that they already have all of the tools to do this. They just stopped doing it. When people first meet someone, they make a lot of effort on their appearance, flirting, conversation, going out on dates etc. Then over time people get too comfortable and stop trying...

It's great to be comfortable in a relationship and when dating, but you need to always be doing the things that you did at the start to keep the spark alive. Going on dates to new places, making an effort sexually in the bedroom, having those deep conversations, making an effort with your appearance, flirting etc. These are the things that are fun and exciting and will keep the spark alive in the relationship.

If you stop doing these things that you did at the start of the relationship, the sex life will disappear, the relationship will become boring, and before you know it, you'll be in a sexless, boring relationship and you'll feel like they are your friend and not your lover.

So basically, keep doing all of the things you did when you first met them, and I 100% guarantee that the spark will never go. It's a simple tip, but one that many people forget to do...

Ask yourself, 'Is this person emotionally mature enough to date me?'

This is a question that you need to ask yourself whenever you are dating someone. You don't want to be dating somebody who is levels below you when it comes to emotional maturity. If you do, this opens up a world of problems.

When you both have an argument, and they handle things in an immature way, is this really the type of relationship that you want to be in?

When you need your boundaries respected and they are more worried about their own self-interests, then you know that they aren't emotionally mature enough for you.

And one of the biggest signs of maturity levels is, do they show good levels of empathy? If they don't and you do, then it could be very hard for you to relate to each other in different situations.

There are many different ways that people display emotional maturity, and many different ways they show their lack of it.

Really look within yourself and evaluate your own levels of emotional maturity and observe if the person you're dating is on the same level as you. If they aren't, then it's time to let that person go. But if they are, then it's a very good green flag.

Get comfortable with saying 'NO'!

Many of us don't use the word 'No' enough. If you are dating the correct way, I guarantee that you'll be saying 'No' a lot more than you will be saying 'Yes'!

By saying 'No' you are protecting your peace, time, and energy. Saying 'No' eliminates people you are not compatible with. It stops you spending time with people that you don't want to spend time with. It stops you from being in uncomfortable situations. Saying 'No' commands respect from people.

When you meet the right person who treats you the correct way, you'll be thankful that you said 'No' to everyone who wasn't them!

So, get comfortable saying 'No' to people, and your dating life will be much easier!

This is your love story... Enjoy it!

This is your love story... Enjoy it! There will be ups and there will be downs. You will meet some bad people and you will meet some good people. You will have some bad stories and you will have some amazing stories. This is all part of the process. Accept it for what it is and truly enjoy the process.

At times you might want to give up, but if you do, you could be stopping yourself from meeting the love of your life the next day! Everyone's story is unique. This is your story, and that makes it something very special.

Every good story throughout history is full of tales of people overcoming obstacles, meeting different types of people, growing as a person themselves, and then living happily ever after. If the book started at 'And she lived happily ever after', then that's a very boring story. Instead, embrace the growth within yourself that will you find when you fully embrace the dating experience.

I honestly hope that you meet the love of your life on your next date, but if you don't, it's just part of your journey until you do meet the love of your life.

When you're older and you are with your forever partner, you'll look back and be thankful for everything you have gone through because it led you to them.

Remember this… In love you have only got to find 'The One' once in your life…

Epilogue

My goal within this book is to of helped you navigate the world of dating. Now that you have a better understanding of how to date, build attraction, know the red and green flags to lookout for, how to flirt, and much more… you must now apply this to your own love life.

I promise you that now you have learnt and understood these tips and pieces of advice, your dating journey will become much smoother and much more enjoyable. You will know exactly what to do when dating!

For example, you'll be talking to people and notice them displaying some body language that shows they are attracted to you, and you'll think to yourself, 'Ah, that was in *Her Dating Coach*, I know exactly what that means!'

Or you'll be texting someone and you won't be confused anymore on what to say or do. Instead, you'll come across as smooth, in control, know how to build attraction, and get that date!

Another time, you'll be on a date with a guy, and you'll notice a red flag that you wouldn't have noticed before and know exactly what it means and where it is heading. On the other hand, you'll know exactly when a man has an abundance of green flags, and you'll know you are on a date with someone who could be the one!

The more you know about dating, the better. Before you know it, you'll be the one giving your friends advice. They will be telling you about some guy that they are dating and what he has said or done, and you'll know exactly what is going on, and you will know the correct path for your friend to take for them to be happier in their dating life.

It is really a wonderful thought for me to think that this book will help you find the love of your life. My goal is to help as many people as possible with their love life.

By helping you I am sure that you will pass this knowledge on to others, creating a ripple effect where people are happier and more successful when dating and in their relationships.

Thank you so much for reading this book and may you forever be happy and blessed in your love life...

'Love is like a game of chess. If you rush it, a piece of you will be taken. If you take your time and make the right moves, you will get the King you've always wanted.'

Sincerely,
Your Professional Dating Coach
Jacob Lucas

Made in the USA
Middletown, DE
09 April 2023

28513262R00144